IN DEFENSE OF MYSTICAL IDEAS
*Support for Mystical Beliefs from
a Purely Theoretical Viewpoint*

Tobias Chapman

Problems in Contemporary Philosophy
Volume 12
The Edwin Mellen Press
Lewiston/ Lampeter/ Queenston

Library of Congress Cataloging-in-Publication Data

Chapman, Tobias.
   In defense of mystical ideas : support for mystic beliefs from a
purely theoretical viewpoint / by Tobias Chapman.
      p.   cm. -- (Problems in contemporary philosophy ; vol. 12)
   Includes index.
   ISBN   0-88946-340-9
   1. Mysticism.   2. Meaning (Philosophy) I. Title. II. Series.
B828.C46   1989
210--dc19

88-32655
CIP

This is volume 12 in the continuing series
Problems in Contemporary Philosophy
Volume 12 ISBN 0-88946-340-9
PCP Series ISBN 0-88946-325-5

A CIP catalog record for this book
is available from the British Library.

The Edwin Mellen Press
Box 450
Lewiston, NY
USA 14092

The Edwin Mellen Press
Box 67
Queenston, Ontario
CANADA L0S 1L0

The Edwin Mellen Press, Ltd.
Lampeter, Dyfed, Wales,
UNITED KINGDOM SA48 7DY

Printed in the United States of America

TABLE OF CONTENTS

CHAPTER ONE

Introduction

Most scholars of religion, whatever their own personal religious beliefs
may be, agree that within all religions, whether of the "higher" or
allegedly more "primitive" variety, there exists a common core of beliefs,
usually called "mystical." These beliefs are very remote from those which
in the Western world we tend to call common-sensical.

Although this tradition is an exceedingly complex one, many stu-
dents of the subject would agree that there is a *single* tradition, i.e., a set
of beliefs which are common to all mystics whether they be Jewish,
Taoist, Moslem, Catholic, Orthodox, Protestant, or, indeed, have no
formal religious belief or affiliation at all. As well as holding a set of
theoretical or philosophical beliefs, mystics also advocate a set of
practices the aim of which is to engender a psychological state conducive
to religious experience. Most mystical writing seems to be concerned
with the latter rather than the former. Generally speaking, what is
important to mystics is contemplative practice and experience, not
intellectual speculation and ratiocination. In fact, most mystics would
claim that to a very important extent, the content of mystical doctrine
cannot be expressed adequately in linguistic terms nor clearly
understood at all without the appropriate experiences. Hence they
usually emphasize practice rather than theory. The purpose of this book
is to defend certain central mystical ideas from a purely theoretical point
of view. In some respects this task is much less important than that of
providing instruction in the meditative and other practices which may
result in a person's having religious experience, but I am not qualified to
provide such instruction. My aim is to provide arguments which, if
sound (are valid and have true premises), will lend support to the
mystic's claim that his experiences are veridical, that is, they really do
provide knowledge of a reality very different from the one that we
ordinarily experience; or that they provide insight into aspects of reality
which are normally hidden from us. This theoretical task seems to me
worthwhile since, as has often been argued, religious experience is not

self-verifying; it does not, in itself, provide grounds for thinking that mystical beliefs are true. In this introductory chapter I shall first of all give a sketch of the central core of mystical doctrine that I will be arguing for, and discuss some problems of interpretation, and also certain epistemological issues, i.e., problems about the knowledge claims that mystics make.

It is extremely difficult to be precise and succinct or perhaps, in some respects, even intelligible in describing the beliefs which mystics hold in common. This is partly due to the fact that they are normally expressed in the complex symbolism of various, different, religious traditions, and also because beliefs arising from the particular tradition to which the mystic in question belongs are often expressed in the same passages as those which are of a more universal kind. More important than this, however, is the fact that mystical beliefs are very remote from those of common sense and ordinary life especially as these are understood in the West. In this respect, and even in regard to content, according to some authors such as Capra,[1] they are akin to some of the doctrines of modern physics. But, of course, mystical doctrine has a much harder time of it than physics in at least two general respects. First of all, it cannot be scientifically verified in the usual sense. (This remark will be qualified in certain ways later on.) Secondly, physics has a set of precise languages in which it can be expressed, viz., those of mathematics, whereas mysticism and art do not. In fact according to most of the mystics themselves there *cannot* exist a language in which their beliefs can be clearly expressed, although those who have had similar experiences are better able to understand more or less practical allusions to these beliefs.

Bertrand Russell has been as successful as anyone in attempting to state the essential views of mystics in a clear way. He says that when mystics take themselves to be in contact with reality, as such, as opposed to the very narrow slice of it that we ordinarily perceive, they are agreed that reality has four characteristics:

1. There is a better method of gaining knowledge of it than through ordinary sense-perception.

2. There is a "fundamental unity" to all things.

3. Our common-sense view of time is somehow illusory.

4. All evil is "mere appearance."

It should be added that most mystics, though by no means all, are theists of one kind or another. They are also normally monotheists, but with regard to this latter point some authors have claimed to perceive important differences between mystics of different types, the "type" being dependent usually on the religious tradition to which the mystic adheres. Zaehner,[2] for example, distinguishes three main kinds of mysticism. (1) Nature mysticism: here the mystic claims to perceive the unity of all things with the self; the distinction between subject and object disappears. William James, for example, describes the following experience. "I was impelled to kneel down, this time before the illimitable ocean, symbol of the Infinite. I felt that I prayed as I had never prayed before, and know now what prayer really is: to return from the solitude of individuation into the consciousness of unity with all that is, to kneel down as one that passes away, and to rise up as one imperishable."[3] Another beautifully expressed statement of this idea can be found in the writings of the seventeenth century mystic and poet, Thomas Traherne. "You never enjoy the world aright, till the Sea floweth in your veins, till you are clothed with the heavens, and crowned with the stars: and perceive yourself to be the sole heir of the whole world, and more than so, because men are in it who are every one sole heirs as well as you. Till you can sing and rejoice and delight in God ... you never enjoy the world."[4] (2) The second view Zaehner calls "soul mysticism" which is based on an experience of the unity of the self with God (in one of various senses to be discussed later). This is a common theme in Hindu mysticism where the goal of religious practice is often to recognize one's identity with God or the Absolute; "I am Brahman" and "What thou art, that am I."[5] But this, or a very similar idea, occurs also in the writings of Christian mystics, e.g., in Ruysbroeck and Eckhart. Ruysbroeck writes, "...the spirit, in its inmost and highest part, that is, in its naked nature, receives without interruption the impress of its Eternal Archetype, and the Divine rightness; and is an eternal dwelling place of God in which God dwells as an eternal Preserve...."[6] Similarly Eckhart asserts, "God had endowed the soul with his own likeness, which did she not possess she could not be God by grace nor above grace either; whereas in this likeness she is able to attain to being God by grace...."[7] (3) Thirdly, Zaehner distinguishes theistic mysticism which is based on the experience of a transcendent God. The subject of the experience seems somehow united with God but recognizes that God is utterly distinct from him. In the profound medieval English mystical work, *The Cloud of Unknowing*, the individual soul is said to be "oned" with God. Certainly one *can* distinguish between the above sorts of mysticism: some people who have experiences of the first sort reject theism altogether. Zaehner is also presumably correct in stressing that there can be such a thing as false mysticism (Rimbaud[8], for example, rejected the validity of his own mystical experiences); and certainly Zaehner also seems correct in his claim that it is a mark of mystical experience that the subject feels that he has passed beyond all moral obligation, but perhaps only in the sense of no longer having a desire to violate the moral law. However, Zaehner's distinction between *monism* (the view that reality is a unity, that diverse particulars are all manifestations of a single substance) and *theism* (the view that God is a transcendent Being) may have no application in this context, although of course, it is a perfectly valid distinction. Zaehner contrasts the Christian view that in mystical experience a person can be "oned" with God with the Hindu view (as expressed, e.g., by Sankara) that one's soul is identical with God. (Zaehner as a Roman Catholic favours the former.) Similarly, a nature mystic *might*, but need not, espouse the view that God and nature are identical, i.e., he *may* interpret his experience as evidence for pantheism. But it is equally true that orthodox Catholic theologians such as St. Thomas Aquinas allow that God, though transcendent, is everywhere, and that the soul or "part of" the soul can have a "unity" with God, without, of course, *being* God. As St. Paul himself says, "I live, now not I, but Christ liveth in me." Thus, although I would accept the distinctions which Zaehner makes here, I want to emphasize a very different point about them, viz., that it is perfectly possible for the beliefs to which these different types of mystical experience give rise *to be consistent with one another* and with the content of virtually all religions, including orthodox Christianity. A nature mystic can, for example perfectly well experience God-in-nature directly while acknowledging that God is also infinite and transcendent. Similarly a mystic whose experiences are purely of God as transcendent, as wholly other, can also acknowledge the possibility of perfectly valid mystical experiences of the divine in nature, at least if they are given a religious as well as a purely psychological interpretation; they need not be false in that they would involve an affirmation of pantheism. But whether this apparent contradiction is his considered view or not, it does not seem, to me to be correct. Since God can be taken to be *both* immanent and transcendent, as most Christians believe, nature-mysticism simply does not logically entail pantheism. Thomas Traherne is a good example of a mystic whose experiences appear to have been of all of the three sorts which Zaehner mentions. In this book, in any case, we will be concerned with the rational defence of the core of mystical faith and not with the delineation of criteria for identifying false mysticism.[9]

The first feature of mystical belief that Russell mentioned was the idea that there is a type of knowledge which is quite different from common-sensical or scientific knowledge. It does not involve any inductive or deductive (mathematical) reasoning, but rather consists of a direct "insight" into the nature of some feature of reality. Of course scientific, psychological and mathematical truths are often arrived at, especially amongst adepts of the disciplines involved, by some intuitive non rational means, but these sorts of truths can and must be independently verified by experiment in the scientific case and deductive proof in the mathematical, whereas mystical beliefs cannot be. There is a further mystical doctrine that results from this, viz., that the truths at which the mystic arrives are *ineffable*, they cannot be adequately expressed in ordinary or, in fact, any language. This belief obviously presents extremely difficult philosophical problems. I have devoted two chapters to the attempt to resolve some of them. Here I simply mention the view and will give some quotations to illustrate it, and also to illustrate the other beliefs which Russell mentions. A very famous expression of ineffability is the opening lines of the beautiful treatise of Chinese mysticism, the *Tao Te Ching:*

>"There are ways but the Way is uncharted;
>
>There are names but not nature in words:
>
>Nameless indeed is the source of creation."[10]

Similarly, Nicholas of Cusa, the fifteenth century philosopher, mathematician and mystic, in his book *The Vision of God (Visio Dei)* says, "I observed how needful it is for me to enter into the darkness and to admit the coincidence of opposites, beyond all the grasp of reason and there to seek the truth where impossibility meeteth me."[11]

The second mystical doctrine that Russell mentions is the belief that there is a "fundamental unity" to all things. This can, of course, be interpreted in several different ways. It is not, however, ambiguous, I think, but is rather a kind of summary of several different, though closely connected, mystical views about the nature of reality. This will be discussed in more detail in the chapter on the subject. Here I will just provide some representative quotes. In the Hindu scripture the *Bhagavad Gita*, xi:13, Krishna, an Incarnation of God, reveals himself as such to the mortal hero of the book, Arjuna; Arjuna then saw "the whole body of the God of gods."[12] According to a Tantric Buddhist, "The external world and [the Buddhist's] inner world are for him only two sides of the same fabric, in which the threads of all forces and of all events, of all forms of consciousness and of their objects, are woven into an inseparable net of endless mutually conditioned relations."[13] It is normally held by mystics that man's real aim is to regain this unity on a direct experiential level.

Thirdly, the mystics generally hold that our common-sense view of time is somehow illusory. The ancient Greek idealist philosopher Parmenides, in describing "the one," the essence of reality which he thought could be deduced on purely logical grounds says, "it never was, nor shall it be ever; for it is now, together, all, one, continuous."[14] A very famous and beautiful statement of the experience of timelessness occurs in Proust. Marcel, the hero of *Remembrance of Things Past*, has returned depressed and fatigued from an afternoon walk and his aunt gives him a cup of tea and 'un petite madeleine.'

"He dips the biscuit into his tea and raises it to his lips. But at that very moment when the mouthful mixed with the crumbs of the cake touched my palate, I shuddered, as I took note of the strange things that were going on inside me. An exquisite pleasure had invaded me, -- isolated, with no idea of what its cause might be. Immediately it had made the vicissitudes of life indifferent, its disasters inoffensive, its brevity illusory, -- in much the same way as love operates, filling me with a precious essence: or rather this essence was not *in* me, it *was* me. I had ceased to feel
mediocre, contingent or mortal."[15]

And much later he says concerning certain images of Combray and Venice,
"In truth the being which was then tasting this impression in me tasted it in what was common between a day long past and now, in what was outside time: and this being would only appear at a time when, through one of these identities between the present and the past, it could exist in the only atmosphere in which it could live and enjoy the essence of the thing, that is to say outside time."[16]

The view that time is unreal (or dependent on the peculiar way in which our consciousness usually apprehends reality) is admittedly a doctrine of dubious intelligibility, by which I mean that it is totally at variance with our ordinary experience and common-sense beliefs, and with the presuppositions of ordinary language. This problem will be discussed to the extent that this is possible in the chapters on time and on meaning. The doctrine also has more than one interpretation, but as in the case of other mystical views, I think that more than one of these is intended. It could be taken to mean that the object of the mystical subject's experience is experienced as timeless, but that the subject himself is not, like the ordinary experience of observing a static array of some kind, e.g., the frames of a film. Here we have a temporal consciousness observing a non-temporal static representation of a temporal series of events. But this cannot be correct since the subject is always described by mystics as merging in some sense with the object of his apprehension; so that if the one is timeless so is the other. The "content" of the doctrine might be given by saying that although reality itself has no temporal properties we apprehend it as if it did. (Time comes from imposed distinctions.) A possible analogy is this: if we were moved swiftly along a stationary film strip in such a way that we had no perception of our motion then we would see the events depicted on the film as if they were actually occurring and we were stationary. (I should would like to stress that this is *only* an analogy.)

Two scientific comparisons are often given to help explain the idea of time's unreality. The first is that in the special theory of relativity absolute time is unreal to this extent, that the length of the temporal interval between any two events is relative to the frame of reference chosen. Secondly, if, relative to a particular frame, two events are not causally connectible because a signal travelling between them would have a velocity greater than the speed of light, then, relative to that frame they have no particular temporal order at all, i.e., we cannot say which is before the other. The invariant quantity in special or restricted relativity is the spatio-temporal interval obtained by combining ordinary spatial and temporal measurements. The second analogy is not based on a universally accepted interpretation of a scientific theory as the first is. It is the view that quantum mechanics can be interpreted as establishing that temporal order is a statistical phenomenon occurring only at the macroscopic level of perceptible objects arising out of a temporal "chaos" at the microscopic level where the fundamental concepts are not those of space and time.[17] Unfortunately, the first is sometimes expressed in such a way as to suggest that modern physics has proven that time is unreal, at least to the extent that any scientific theory can be taken as proven. But this is not so: if special relativity is true then either absolute time does not exist or the idea has no application. At best this shows that *some*, apparently common-sensical, temporal ideas are incorrect, e.g., that there is such a thing as worldwide simultaneity -- that there is some unambiguous way, which does not involve delineating a frame of reference, in which events which are widely separated in space can be temporarily ordered. There is no such way of ordering events in special relativity, but in that theory some "ordinary" temporal concepts still have application, i.e., the theory does not assert that time is unreal. If, for example, two events are causally connectible then the one is temporally prior to the other relative to every frame of reference. T

here is a further difficulty with the idea of using scientific theories to support mystical views. It suggests that mystics and scientists are describing identical realities (or the same aspects of "the real" world) whereas this is, of course, arguable; the mystic has an insight into aspects of reality which transcend the physical world, in part at least. (A pantheist might disagree.) In this book, I will try to argue that time is unreal in a very straightforward sense, viz., that the concept is contradictory. The question of the ontological status of space seems to be more complex.

The last mystical thesis that Russell mentions is the unreality of evil. This is in many ways the most complex of the mystical doctrines and the hardest to interpret. Russell takes it to be an expression of the now very familiar (but not necessarily correct) idea that values are "subjective," that they are not among the "objective facts" of the "real world." Part of the difficulty here can be illustrated from a passage in Wittgenstein's *Tractatus* which might seem to be expressing the same idea as Russell's: "If there is any value that does have value, it must lie outside the whole sphere of what happens and is the case."[18] But Wittgenstein's view is that value, or at least what he later called "absolute value," is ineffable and transcendental, rather than dependent on human consciousness or in some other way "subjective." This is probably also partly what the mystic means. Some mystics also mean that a mystical experience can place one "beyond morality" either in a bad sense (that he is no longer required to help the needy etc.) or in the sense that his experiences leave him with no desire to commit immoral acts. I suppose that the latter is a desirable state to be in providing that it does not involve inflation or self-deception of some kind. Lastly, some mystics appear to believe that there literally is no evil, that what appears to be evil is necessary (i.e., a good, perhaps to provide a contrast or background against which the good can be seen to be good). This is the one area in which it seems to me the mystics may simply be mistaken. Alternatively it may be impossible to understand their views here without having had the relevant experience.

Another typical mystical view which Russell does not discuss separately is that the empirical or phenomenal ego or self (the human person which was the object of study in old-fashioned scientific psychology) is not identical with the "real self." Presumably Russell does not discuss this specifically because it can be treated as part of the doctrine of the "unity of all things." Some of our earlier quotations could be interpreted in this way.

I do not wish to modify Russell's analysis, but I do wish to make some further initial comments on these doctrines and their relation to the argument of this book, and to mention some further doctrines which are also typical of mysticism. It is impossible, I believe, to argue *directly* for the truth of the first claim that mystics have a special kind of knowledge. It is true that many religious teachers have given instructions as to how to attain a mystical or similar religious experience and some authors have tried to draw an analogy between this fact and the fact that a scientist can provide instructions on how to obtain direct evidence for some esoteric scientific theory (e.g., the lengthening of the life-time of mesons with a high velocity as evidence for the time-dilation effect of the special theory of relativity). But this analogy does not work. The results of scientific experimentation can be independently verified in various ways and thus provide a rational way of arriving at approximations to the truth. This is not true of mystical procedures: they do not provide a method for ascertaining facts which can be independently checked but, rather, provide a recipe for having certain experiences, including, to be sure the *feeling that* certain beliefs are absolutely true. But of course the psychological feeling of certainty does not guarantee truth and can, in fact, attach itself to the most preposterous beliefs. Hence, although I believe that the core of mystical belief is true, I do not think that this can be confirmed by direct appeal to mystical experience itself without some sort of independent evidence.

A slightly different but related argument for the truth of the results of mystical experience has been proposed by the distinguished English philosopher, C. D. Broad. This is simply that mystics generally agree as to what facts their subjective experience gives credence to. In the end, argues Broad, ordinary knowledge is in the same epistemological boat, being based on our common perceptions which are ultimately private and subjective (i.e., only *you* can have your experiences of colour, shape, sound, etc.). In some ways this argument raises very complex philosophical issues, particularly concerning the status of skepticism, which would require a book in themselves. For our purposes here we need only observe that our ordinary knowledge claims are always potentially subject to a very thorough, and sometimes complicated, checking procedure. Except in odd or unfortunate circumstances a person normally relies on his memory, eyesight, hearing, etc., to provide ordinary knowledge about the world. But any proposition about past events, the colour and shape of (ordinary, macroscopic) objects, about what was said, etc,. can be elaborately checked if the proposition asserts something which can be known at all. And this is precisely what is not true of mystical assertions. I want to mention two qualifications concerning what I have said here which, again, cannot be adequately dealt with in the scope of the present work. The first is the respects in which, and the extent to which, what counts as *knowledge* can be construed as socially relative. If the answer is, "to a large extent," and if mystics as a group can be thought of as forming a "society" then, within that society, mystical beliefs would seem to constitute "knowledge." I do not, myself, agree with this view, though its considered refutation might be much more difficult than it appears to be. However, I'm fairly certain that Broad would not agree with it either; so we need not pursue the matter here. The second, and very serious consideration, is this. Mystical experience can have a very salutary effect on the subject who has it. Whether or not this can be construed as evidence for the truth of mystical beliefs is a fairly complex problem. But in the present context, the main problem is that *false* beliefs can *appear*, at least, *usually over a relatively short period of time,* to have salutary effects also. A notorious example would be someone who embraces

Freudianism or some other psychological theory more or less as a religion. For a time this can give the convert a wonderful feeling of power -- he has, after all, an explanation for everything. The bubble, however, tends to burst fairly quickly.

Given, therefore, that I do not believe that mystical experience can provide direct evidence for the truth of mystical beliefs, my approach will be, rather, to provide independent arguments for these beliefs on logical and philosophical grounds.

The second doctrine on Russell's list was the "unity of all things." This doctrine covers a lot of ground and is particularly difficult to elucidate verbally or theoretically, although for those who have experienced it directly what it denotes is apparently perfectly lucid. Sometimes it is taken to mean that every finite thing is an "aspect" of some Infinite Being (God or nature). Other authors mean by it no more than the fact that God is in all things and that all creation is dependent on Him or Her, or That-which-is. Some nature-mystics understand it only as asserting a thesis which is quite plausible on non-mystical grounds, that all events are to some degree causally connected. It is also related to the view (beautifully expressed by Meister Eckhart) that each human soul is an infinitesimal "part" ("spark" is Eckhart's term) of the infinite God. Hindu mystics seem to hold further that all these are identical with each other and with God (Brahmin). What I wish to argue for here are the related, theoretical, views which can provide a rational or philosophical foundation for part of the religious doctrines. The question of the transcendental or metaphysical subject of experience will be dealt with in a separate section. The two doctrines to be defended are, (a) the relativity of identity (that "two" things can be identical relative to one concept and not identical relative to another) and the implications of this, and the related view, (b) that space is "unreal." The reason I have put the latter word in quotes is that it notoriously has quite different, but related, senses. I will also argue, thirdly, for the thesis that *time* is unreal. Here the argument for unreality is based on the idea that the notion of time is logically contradictory, whereas in the case of space I do not intend anything as strong, or seemly at variance with common sense, as in the case of the view that time is unreal. Lastly, most, but not all, mystics are theists. My approach to this doctrine will be to try to defend a very simple version of the traditional ontological argument for the existence of God. Initially at least, virtually everyone, myself included, finds this argument intuitively unsatisfactory inasmuch as it passes from premises concerning only considerations about the (or a) concept of God to a conclusion which asserts His existence. As I try to argue, it appears possible, however, to construct, or rather reconstruct, a sound version of this argument, i.e., a valid argument with true premises, which has as its conclusion that God exists. It is also an interesting, but logically very odd, feature of this argument that its conclusion, though very difficult to interpret, accords precisely with what mystics generally say about God or about the God-Head or the "ground of being."

14

Notes to Chapter One

1.   Fritjof Capra, *The Tao of Physics, An Exploration of the Parallels Between Modern Physics and Eastern Mysticism* (Berkeley: Shambhala, 1975).

2.   R.C. Zaehner, *Mysticism Sacred and Profane* (Oxford: Oxford University Press, 1969).

3.   Wm. James, *The Varieties of Religious Experience*, pp. 394-395 (quote in Zaehner, p. 38).

4.   Thomas Traherne, *Centuries of Meditations*, Bk. I: 27-31, as quoted in F. C. Happold, *Mysticism*, (Penguin, 1970), pp. 371-372.

5.   Quoted in Zaehner p. 33.

6.   The Blessed John Ruysbroeck, *The Adornment of the Spiritual Marriage*, trans., C. A. Wynshenk, Bk. II, 57 (from Happold, p. 285).

7.   Meister Eckhart, *Tractate II* in the Pfeiffer edition of his works (from Happold, pp. 274, 275).

8.   There is a very interesting discussion of Rimbaud in Zaehner, Chapter IV.

9.   Rudolf Otto in his *Mysticism, East and West* provides us with a detailed study of the, perhaps at first astonishing, parallels between Eckhart's Christian thought and that of the Hindu mystic, Sankara. But it should be mentioned, in light of what Zaehner says, that some of Eckhart's writings were condemned by the Catholic Church. That some mysticism has, on occasion, been mixed in with gross superstition, and that some mystical practices appear odd or worse, is undeniable. Examples may be found in

Ben-Ami Scharfstein's book, *Mystical Experiences*, Penguin, 1974. In general, experiences identified as "mystical" can be many things, e.g., (a) outright delusion, (b) a return to natural innocence or an "infantile" state (a psychoanalytic view which, if it is intended as a criticism of mystical experience, commits the traditional logical fallacy of *ad hominem)*; (c) a direct insight into the nature of subatomic physical reality (on which see Capra's book mentioned in Note 1 above); (d) an initial stage of genuine mystical experience; (e) partially or wholly an experience of God as immanent in all things; (f) an insight into the "archetypal self," or (g) some other aspect of the "collective unconscious," (h) some combination of these (as an experience can have both delusory and veridical elements); (i) the culmination of a psychological process of "integration" or "individuation" (in this connection Zaehner in Chapter IV has a very interesting discussion of Proust), and so on. But as previously mentioned, I am not here interested in classifying mystical experiences of different sorts or in identifying false mysticism, but only in providing independent philosophical arguments for what I take to be the common core of mystical belief.

10. Lao Tzu, *Tao Te Ching*, trans. R. B. Blakney (New York and Scarborough, Ontario: 1955), p. 53.

11. Happold, p. 336.

12. Happold, p. 30.

13. Quotation from Capra, p. 143.

14. Zaehner, p. 47.

15. Proust, *A la Recherche due Temps Perdu* (Paris: Bibliotheque de la Pleiade, Gallimard, 1954), vol. i, p. 45. This, and the other quotations from Proust, are in Zaehner's translation, pp. 52-56.

16

16.   Proust, vol. iii, p. 871 (Zaehner, p. 56).

17.   The noted philosopher of science Hans Reichenbach believed this to be so and provides an argument for it in his book *The Direction of Time* (University of California Press, 1970). Roughly speaking the argument is that since, following the physicist Feynmann, positrons can be construed mathematically as electrons "going backwards in time," a temporal order cannot be defined on the subatomic level. See also E. J. Zimmermann, "The Macroscopic Nature of Space-Time," *American Journal of Physics*, Vol. 3O 1962: pp. 97-105.

18.   Ludwig Wittgenstein, *Tractatus Logico-Philosophicus* London: Routledge and Kegan Paul, 1961, 6.41, p. 145.

Scholarly Note to Chapter I

The purpose of this work is not to provide a thoroughgoing scholarly analysis of all those very diverse religious traditions which have been labelled "mystical." The upshot of such a study would probably be, as Steven Katz remarks, [1] to "disabuse scholars of the preconceived notion that all mystical experience is the same or similar." I am *not* claiming that all mystical experiences are alike in some way. It is, in fact, unclear to me how such a phenomenological analysis would proceed. Nor am I claiming that behind the obscure language which is the expression of religious experience there lies a doctrinal purity encapsulated in the five religious theses discussed in this chapter. All I am claiming is that these five theses seem to be common to many mystical traditions and that, although they admit of various interpretations, the ambiguities involved are not irresolvable or overwhelming, reducing in effect to a mere similarity of words. In fact, were it established by an historian or sociologist of religion that the five theses discussed here were held by a tiny minority of mystics only, this would in no way undermine the present project. I am concerned here with defending the idea that these theses are true, not in establishing who did or did not hold them and in what form.

---

[1]   Steven T. Katz, "Language, Epistemology and Mysticism," in Steven T. Katz, Ed., *Mysticism and Philosophical Analysis*, London: Sheldon Press, 1978, pp. 22-24.

CHAPTER TWO

Mysticism, Metalogic and the Unsayable

In a famous passage in the *Tractatus*, 4.126, Wittgenstein says the following concerning a distinction he makes between what he calls *formal* as opposed to *real* concepts:

"We can now talk about formal concepts, in the same sense that we speak of formal properties. (I introduce this expression in order to exhibit the source of the confusion between formal concepts and concepts proper, which pervades the whole of traditional logic.)

When something falls under a formal concept as one of its objects, this cannot be expressed by means of a proposition. Instead it is shown in the very sign for this object. (A name shows that it signifies an object, a sign for a number that it signifies a number, etc.)

Formal concepts cannot in fact be represented by means of a function, as concepts proper can."

Some examples of formal pseudo-concepts are the concepts of concept itself, predicate, function, object, the relation between a proposition and reality i.e., for the *Tractatus*, the picturing relation, which will be discussed in more detail later. Examples of proper concepts would be things like *red, five*, and technical ideas like that of *low entropy* in physics or *completeness* in logic. In some cases it is hard to tell which category a concept would fall into, e.g., in the case of "denumerable infinity" or the notion of colour or force. This does not however obliterate the distinction. Sometimes Wittgenstein puts the point in this way, that a formal concept attempts to express an internal property of a symbol, i.e., to express how the relevant sign is used, but he argues that, although this is obviously something which can be learned, it is not something that can be explicitly stated. It might be thought that this doctrine is just a dogmatic result of the *picture theory of meaning* (which will be explained shortly) on the grounds that such propositions as those given in the list below do not seem to be pictures of facts and hence, that Wittgenstein is simply asserting that they are formal propositions, so as to avoid the implication that the picturing theory is false, that there are genuine propositions which are not pictures. Consider the following statements:

A. The quantifiers in logic are second-order concepts.
B. The *square root* of is a function, whereas "four" is a name.
C. A chair is a material object.

These assertions obviously employ what the *Tractatus* calls "formal concepts"; here the idea of a concept itself (in A), a function (in B) and of a material object (in C). Hence, according to the early Wittgenstein, these assertions would not express genuine propositions although they certainly *appear* to provide us with a kind of abstract information. When Wittgenstein wrote the *Tractatus* he advocated a relatively simple picturing theory of language according to which authentic empirical propositions are formal pictures of possible facts. If a proposition is true it is a picture of an actual fact. The relatively complex propositions which are ordinarily used in natural languages are certainly *not* pictures in any obvious sense. The *Tractatus* view is that they really are, nonetheless, pictures, inasmuch as they are complex truth-functions of atomic propositions, the latter being literally representations of the atomic facts which they are about. (A complex proposition is a truth-function of simpler propositions when its *truth-value* is a function of the simpler propositions of which it is composed. The logic presupposed in the *Tractatus* is a standard two-valued one, i.e., only two truth-values, true and false are allowed. Then the simplest example of a true truth-functional proposition would be 'p and q' where 'p' and 'q' are true. Another example would be 'not-p' which is true if p is false, and false if p is true.)

It might be thought that Wittgenstein's denial that such sentences as A, B and C above are really propositions simply resulted from his narrow and dogmatic espousal of the picture-theory of sentential meaning, that is to say, having observed that such statements as A, B and C cannot possibly be construed as pictures of anything, he simply denied that they were authentic propositions at all. However, the two doctrines (the picturing theory of meaning and the distinction between formal and proper concepts) can be disentangled. The argument for the distinction between formal and real concepts is quite powerful, while there appears to be practically no argument for the picture theory at all, although it has a strong intuitive appeal. It is also arguable that Wittgenstein adhered to the distinction between formal and proper concepts in his later philosophy, but not to the picturing theory of meaning, and certainly not to the view that there are elementary propositions. Hence the doctrine of formal concepts is not just a dogmatic consequence of the probably over-simplified and partially false picturing theory. This might be usefully contrasted with Wittgenstein's attitude in the *Tractatus* towards modality (i.e., the concepts of possibility and necessity). He seems to reject the Aristotelian idea of a kind of necessity which attached to propositions about the past simply on the grounds that they cannot be pictures; so *here* his views *are* just a dogmatic result of the picture theory.

To understand what Wittgenstein has in mind let us consider some further examples.

    D. "x is a variable."

    E. "4 is a number."

    F. "'4' is a numeral."

    G. "'Red' is a predicate."

    H. "Identity is a relation."

    I. "'Identity' is a word denoting a relation."

If these are to be genuinely informative propositions it must be possible for them to be false, but this is obviously not literally so in the case of D, E, and F, for we are not here talking about language (construed as something observable) but about the actual things concerned, perhaps as revealed by the uses of the marks. Of course in a kind of trivial sense F, G, and I could be false and in fact Carnap objected to Wittgenstein's views on the grounds that statements like D, E, and I could be translated into the so-called *formal mode* of speech, that is, one involving only references to words; in which case they could be false. An example of the sort of thing Carnap has in mind would be this. I could be rewritten in the formal (as opposed to material) mode of speech as, "The word 'identity' is used in the English language to refer to a certain relation, usually between numbers." This statement is certainly contingent and hence could be false (if, simply, a different word were used in English for the relevant relation). I'll return to this point later. F for example is false of Latin, G is false where "Red" is used as the name of a person, and we could invent a language where the identity sign was used for the number two. But this is just to say that the signs, that is the marks or tokens, not the real symbols, have different usages; "4" and "red", etc., usually reproduces a sign on the tacit assumption of its use as a symbol. It follows that these sentences are not genuinely informative for one would already have to understand how "four," "red," etc., are used in order to understand what is referred to in the relevant propositions; of course one might not be familiar with the vocabulary of "variable" and "function", etc., but a working knowledge of the language would be necessary in order to grasp their use. They are therefore to be contrasted with technical terms like "positron," "tachyon" or "consistency proof," the meaning of which can be explained in a relatively straight-forward way. With regard to the above remark about Carnap, we might attempt to avoid this difficulty by the semantical device of introducing proper names of the terms in question. However, as the logician Reach pointed out long ago (*Journal of Symbolic Logic*, 1938, pages 97 to 111), supposing one says,

1. "Alpha is the name of "4" (a name),"
2. "Alpha is the name of a numeral."

To clearly understand (1) is already to understand (2) since we must grasp that the "4" referred to in (1) is the name of a number, and not, for example, an artistic flourish. Even if we allow reproduction of the term in question it cannot be construed as a proper name, it must be understood as a *description* referring to a particular use. Otherwise it would be correct to infer from the true statement, "'Red' is a predicate" that the letters r, e, d, in the word "predatory" name a property.

Similarly consider one of the things that is essential to Tarski's famous semantical theory of truth, viz., the material condition that must be satisfied by any such theory, that "'s' is true if and only if s" where "s" is an ordinary true-or-false proposition. If one is to understand this, "s" (in quotes) must *reproduce* a relevant sentence, not just name it. Strictly speaking I should say that *"s"* is an *abbreviation* for a reproduction of the relevant proposition. But I can only pick out a relevant sentence if I know what it means; and to know what "s" means is to know what it is for it to be true. Hence the condition cannot be informative. This is discussed in a bit more detail below. (If we disentangle this view of Wittgenstein's from the picture theory, then although it applies to some of the procedures of formal semantics, it appears not to apply to all metamathematical and metalogical procedures for the following reason. One can use a certain propositional calculus, for example, without knowing that it's consistent or complete or decidable or even what the later terms mean. Hence the proof, for example, that first order logic is not decidable is certainly in some sense informative, in fact for most people it is very surprising and counter-intuitive.)

Hence we all in a sense know things which cannot be significantly and informatively asserted: in this case, for example, the distinction between name, variable and function. There are pseudo-propositions according to Wittgenstein which *show* what would be true if they could be meaningfully asserted. "Show" (zeigen) is a technical term for Wittgenstein: a poem, a piece of music or a painting may show us some aspect of reality which cannot be described in literal language. This partly explains Wittgenstein's remark at 6.522, "There indeed exist things that cannot be put into words," and in 6.13, "logic is transcendental." As already remarked, a version of this doctrine seems to have been held by the later Wittgenstein as well. For example, in the *Philosophische Bemerkungen* Section 31 (written about 1930), he says there is a sense in which the employment of language cannot be taught namely by talking about it, since one would have to already, tacitly or otherwise, understand the language in question (or a very similar language) in order to grasp the sense of the second-order language used to describe it.

An important example of a formal concept is the concept of linguistic picturing or modelling. In *Tractatus* 2.172 Wittgenstein says, for example, "A model cannot however model a form of modelling; but displays it." Admittedly a model "A" cannot itself state its connection to A but one is (wrongly) inclined to say, another model "A" could be used to state the connection between the model "A" and A. The reason models of the *connection between* thought and reality are impossible is that we would have to isolate in reality the fact A independently of language, and then state how "A" is connected with it. But it is clearly impossible to isolate A independently of language, and then state how "A" is connected with it since it is impossible to isolate A except by means of a model (linguistic or conceptual) and so we would again have to just see the connection between this model and reality, or proceed *ad infinitum.* Consider the example of objects arranged on a table so that one set represents a fact in the world and another set a model, the arrangement of the objects of which is intended to express a logical form. The "logical form" according to the *Tractatus* consists in its having a sufficient number of constituents and sufficient logical multiplicity to depict the fact in question. Representational content is presumably given by the intention of the user of the model to (a) give its constituents reference, (b) make the arrangement depict (not denote) the particular type of fact in question and (c) assert what the model depicts. (Denotation is a quite different relation, e.g., the relation which holds between a proper name or a numeral and their respective objects.) It looks wrongly as if we can represent the relation between "A" and A by means of the following picture (for example - there are other possibilities):

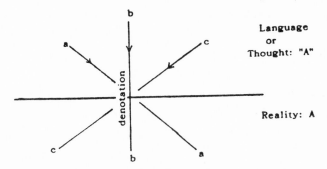

But that this is really a subtle delusion can be seen in several ways.

(1) Note first of all the A above is not a fact but is itself a picture of a fact; so that although one can grasp what is meant by saying "A" pictures A quite readily, the relation between A and reality has not been stated or explained in any way.

(2) Secondly, suppose one claims that the fact he is talking about is that very arrangement of letters pictured on the page. This will easily produce the feeling that one has grasped the fact and the proposition independently of one another and pictured their relationship.

But how does one *isolate* the fact A even in the above simple case? The only way is by expressions like "this arrangement of letters here" which is itself a *proposition*, and so the (pseudo-) explanation presupposes that what it is supposed to explain is already understood. There is no hope at all of isolating the fact one intends purely ostensively. For example, consider even a very simple case such as "This bowl is red," and try to precisely indicate the relevant fact without using language, i.e., purely ostensively (e.g., by simply pointing). Clearly this cannot be done -- anyone can easily list at least twenty different propositions which such a gesture might be intended to express.

In understanding a particular language we understand well enough how to coordinate thought and reality but this connection cannot be stated within any particular proposition itself about its own co-ordination with reality, nor can it be informatively stated in a meta-language. What the metalanguage purports to explain or elucidate must already be tacitly understood; the proposition is not really elucidated at all.

This again illustrates at a very fundamental level the difficult notion of the "ineffable." It is something which can be grasped by almost everyone, but not through a conscious discursive intellectual act, since it is not statable in the sense that its content can be informatively conveyed in a language. At least this cannot be done in the same way that empirical and some formal truths (*and* falsehoods) can be expressed.

CHAPTER THREE

The Formal Character of Truth

The purpose of this section is to argue that the idea of truth is a formal concept in Wittgenstein's sense. I'll start out with some rather simple considerations about the notion of truth in general and discuss the apparent philosophical implications of these ideas. Some of the results of modern mathematical logic will then be discussed in relation to these general notions.

As Frege[1] (and Dummett more recently) have argued, it seems that no theory of truth (call it T) can be both, (a) correct, and (b) an explanation of anything, for if the theory, T is correct, it must be true; but what if I don't understand in virtue of what T is true? Then the answer will have to be, T is correct because it satisfies the criteria set out in T; i.e., in order to understand what T explains I must already understand what it would be for T to be true. Hence the theory is impredicative or circular in a vicious sense and cannot be explanatory.

Secondly, we also seem to have either another vicious circle or an infinite regress with respect to *any* theory of truth. The above is a kind of explanatory circle but it's also the case that if we can be sure that the theory T is true because it satisfies the criteria set out in T then we have what is equivalent to a circular argument in traditional logic. On the other hand if we say that T is correct because it satisfies the criteria set out in another theory T′ then of course the question will arise again as to why T′ is correct. This will require a third theory T″ *ad infinitum.*

The correspondence "theory" of truth that, "p" is true if and only if p, as propounded by Plato and Aristotle and in our own time by Russell, is obviously "correct" in a way; but it is rather unclear whether it has any content, for in order for it to have any significance it would have to be possible to state a criterion for the truth of a statement "p" independently of specifying "p's" meaning; but to specify the sense of a proposition "p," is partly at least, to specify it's truth-conditions. In other words it's certainly correct to say that if a proposition "p" is true then there *corresponds* to it in reality a fact p, but this has no explanatory power. One cannot specify "p's" sense without specifying the criteria of its truth; so to add "and it's true if it corresponds to a fact" is to add nothing. (This is to be contrasted with (a) correspondence as correlation of constituents, and (b) correspondence as congruity of form as an explanation of meaning as it occurs in the *Tractatus*.) Therefore, as Michael Dummett has pointed out, all the correspondence theory of truth seems to amount to is the following:

1. "It is true that p if and only if p" and "It is false that p if and only if not p".
2. "A statement is true only if there is a fact 'in the world' corresponding to it."

In Wittgenstein's *Notebooks* there occurs the following remark (3rd of November 1914), "For a proposition to be true does not consist in its having a *particular* relation to reality but in its *really having* a particular relation." The meaning of this rather obscure remark appears to be that in discussing truth what is wanted is not a particular relation, e.g., correspondence, but rather that *some relation or other* should obtain between the proposition in question and a bit of reality, e.g., the relation could be one of the *various* representing relations. What I mean by the latter is this. The fact that the book is on the table could be *represented by the sentence* "The book in on the table" or by a picture like the following:

The relations between these various "pictures" and reality are all quite different. I doubt that anyone could give a finite list of all the possibilities. Similarly at 4.0621 in the *Tractatus* Wittgenstein says, "The propositions p and not-p have opposite sense, but there corresponds to them one and the same reality." Presumably *what* corresponds is an actual or possible fact. In any case this much is clear, that this passage would be incoherent if Wittgenstein subscribed to a simple correspondence theory of truth. Similarly, at 4.063, Wittgenstein rejects the Fregean doctrine that the verb of *any* proposition is "is true" or "is false"; i.e., propositions represent through their verbs, they do not designate bits of reality as Frege seems to have held of true, unasserted propositions. (An "unasserted proposition" is one that occurs in a type of context which makes clear that no claim is being made as to the truth-value of the proposition. An example would be the statement. "He catches the 6:10 train," in the conditional statement, "If he catches the 6:10, then he'll arrive in Toronto on time.") Lastly, on page 25 of the *Notebooks*, Wittgenstein seems clearly to be arguing for the view that I'm trying to defend here, that a so-called theory of truth can only be *shown*; it cannot be explicitly stated in an informative way. Wittgenstein says the following, for example.

"How can I be *told how* the proposition represents? Or can this not be *said* to me at all? And if that is so can I *know* it? If it was supposed to be said to me, then this would have to be done by means of a proposition which could only show it."

We ought now to look at the philosophical relevance for the concept of truth of Goedel's famous incompleteness theorem for formalized recursive arithmetic, first published in 1931[2]. The account given here will of course be very sketchy and over-simplified but will, I believe, preserve part, at least, of the philosophical import of the theorem. But I will not, for example, discuss the relevance of the theorem to the question of platonism vs. nominalism and the existence of synthetic *a priori* propositions. Let formalized arithmetic be designated by the capital letter A. What Goedel essentially proved is that in any system A which is sufficiently powerful to express formal number theory or "arithmetic," it is possible to construct a proposition, call it "G," for the Goedel sentence, such that the Goedel number for G is the same as the Goedel number for the proposition "It is not provable that G." All the other truths of recursive arithmetic will be theorems of the axiomatic system. In a certain, somewhat over-simplified, sense this is the same as saying that the proposition G is equivalent to the proposition that it is not provable that G. Given this equivalence it is quite easy to then deduce the following statements. Theorem I, Part 1: If A is consistent then G is not provable in A. G is however true in a number of respects. Firstly, it is equivalent to the statement, "It's not provable that G" which is obviously true given the above. It also states a true theorem of recursive arithmetic concerning prime numbers. Theorem I, Part 2 states that, if A is consistent, then it is not provable that not G. It follows immediately that in any system of formalized arithmetic there is at least one undecidable statement, i.e., one statement such that neither it nor its negation is provable. But the statement or its negation is true, and hence provability cannot be identified with truth or we would have a contradiction. As we shall see, this is a philosophically significant result. Theorem II states that if A is consistent its consistency cannot be proven within A itself, although A contains a formal equivalent of the statement that A is consistent. (What is meant by the consistency of any formal system S is simply this; S is consistent if and only if it is not possible to deduce within S a theorem and its negation or any other contradiction. A system S is provably consistent if it is possible to provide a proof of the above in a metalanguage *about* S.) We will return to the question of consistency later. It is important to note in this connection that although we have as a truth of logic that either it's provable that p or it's not provable that p, we do not have as a truth of logic that it's provable that p or it's provable that not-p, since p may be undecidable; as in fact Goedel proved was true of some statement in recursive arithmetic on *any* axiomatization of the subject which presupposes Church's thesis. Goedel's result is purely syntactical in that the formalized arithmetic which he works with contains something corresponding to the notion of provable but nothing corresponding to the notion of truth. The observation, for example, that there is at least one truth of recursive number theory which is not provable, is a statement which itself can be made only in the metalanguage, i.e., a partially informal language about the formal language in question.

The Polish mathematician Tarski, using methods similar to Goedel's, extended these results to formal semantics, i.e., to a system that can contain a notion of truth. An uninterpreted purely syntactical formal system makes no reference to anything outside itself. A semantical system (formal or otherwise) does so and thus can contain statements like "'p' is true." Since "true" describes a relation between propositions and something else (normally), it is inherently a semantical as opposed to a syntactical notion. Tarski begins by accepting a version of the simple Aristotelian definition of truth, viz., ("p" is true if and only if p). As already mentioned, it seems to be the case that this material condition is correct but *cannot* be informative. Tarski discusses a different issue as to whether or not the definition is viciously circular and contends that it is not on the grounds that "p" is a name of the proposition p rather than a reproduction of it. As has already been argued, this does not, however, seem to be the case; although it is true that "p" is the name of p, it can succeed in designating the relevent proposition only if in some manner or other it reproduces it. (See also G. E. M. Anscombe, *An Introduction to Wittgenstein's Tractatus*, on Reach's paper in the *Journal of Symbolic Logic*, 1938.) At any rate, Tarski accepts the Aristotelian definition of truth, but he wishes to go beyond it by giving some kind of explication of the concept. He starts off by defining a semantical concept of truth through characterizing the set of true statements in the formal system of number theory, A, mentioned above. He then shows that if the set of true statements in this system coincided one to one with the set of statements which are provable in the system, then a version of the "liar's paradox" could be formulated within the system and render it inconsistent. The paradox referred to, which is a very ancient one, is this. Suppose we have a statement q which is identical with the statement, "The statement q is false." Then if q is true it is false and if it is false it is true. Hence any system in which a statement of this kind can be constructed will turn out to entail an antimony and hence will be inconsistent. But given Goedel's result, that in any recursive arithmetic such a statement as q (which is equivalent to "it's not provable that q") is in fact constructable, it follows that if we identify *true* with *provable* then an inconsistency will always result in the form of a "liar's paradox." Hence, one of the things Tarski pointed out is that it is impossible to adequately define or elucidate the notion of truth within a formalized language by attempting to equate it with provable. The theoretical motivation behind this identification is that the notion of provable can be explained in an absolutely precise and formal way;

hence if "true" could be identified with "provable" the former would be explained as well. But this seems to be the only possible way of explicating it, hence the notion of truth in application to propositions remains elusive. It is important to note in this connection that the nerve of Goedel's and Tarski's work is not the trivial point that not every term in a theory or language can be defined, i.e., that we must accept some set of undefined terms, but that no matter *what* set of undefined terms we do accept there are certain other terms which cannot be defined *at all* in an informative way, in this case *truth*, but also as previously argued, *function, number* and so on. As Tarski himself has pointed out, an exactly analogous result applies to the notion of empirical truth, for it is obvious that there are many empirical truths which are undecidable in the sense that neither they nor their negations are *now* provable by us, and hence here again the intuitive notion of empirical truth cannot be explicated in terms of the (possibly) formal idea of decidable or scientific provability. It might be argued that this claim involves an ambiguity in the word "provable." Any sufficiently clear factual claim is such that either it or its negation is provable *in principle* though, as a matter of contingent fact, we may not now have the means to establish which is, in fact, the case. Suppose, for example, that someone claims that on this very spot, ten thousand years age a cave man killed a wild boar. The idea then is that although there is not *now*, presumably, any means of ascertaining whether this is true or false, it is verifiable or diversifiable "in principle," perhaps, in the sense that someone who was there at the time would have observed the event in question or not done so. But what I want to argue, as against this idea, is that what we are discussing here is factual truth and hence actual provability *at the present time*. Therefore this talk of "provability-in-principle" is quite empty: in the relevant senses of the terms empirical truth and provability cannot be identified with each other any more than can their mathematical counterparts. Lastly, it has become part of common sense to recognize that no (general) scientific theory can be conclusively verified, can be proven to be true, although they can, of course, be falsified. Hence, on the assumption at least that scientific theories are either true or false, we cannot identify truth and provability in this area either.

It is useful now to consider a few general points about the question of consistency. Goedel proved that it is impossible to prove the consistency of number theory using only the tools available within number theory itself. The consistency of arithmetic has however been proven by Gentzen, but the methods which he employs are extremely powerful. Instead of using ordinary mathematical induction, for example, he uses transfinite induction. The methods are in fact so powerful that the proof from an informal point of view may amount to a case of begging the question since the problem of the consistency of the system on which his methods are based is far more acute that the question of the consistency of formalized number theory itself. (For a discussion of this question see H. DeLong, *A Profile of Mathematical Logic*, Section 29.) In general, there is the following problem with all consistency proofs. Virtually all logicians accept an admittedly rather peculiar definition of implication such that any conditional statement, i.e., any statement of the form, if p then q, is true if the antecedent p is false. It follows from this that a contradictory statement, i.e., a statement that reduces to the form p and not p, entails anything whatever. Now suppose we can formulate within a system S itself a statement that S is consistent; let us refer to the latter statement as "C". Then if S is inconsistent C will be provable, since everything is provable (given the above definition of material implication). Hence, if the proof that S is consistent is to have any significance it must *presuppose that S is consistent*; a point, of course, to which Goedel was sensitive. Thus, all we seem to have is that if an axiomatic system is consistent it may be possible to prove it's consistency. It might seem preferable, therefore, in the case of all consistency proofs, to prove the consistency of S from outside S, that is, in another language S_1 about S, but then clearly the problem will always arise as to whether or not S_1 is consistent and so on *ad infinitum*. The best we can hope for is to prove the consistency of S in a system S_1 which is not stronger than S and preferably weaker and more intuitive, but it is not clear that this is really possible (it is formally possible), since given the above argument about reference to propositions, S_1 will, in a sense, "contain" S in that the "name" of any proposition of S can be formulated in S_1 and must actually reproduce it.

The notions of truth and consistency are, of course, importantly related in that a theory which is inconsistent cannot be true. But what we've seen, I hope, in this section is that the notion of truth is elusive in the sense that it cannot be explicated in terms of something more formal or logically more fundamental and that consistency proofs, where they exist at all, are of dubious significance. In general, it seems that the view of the early Wittgenstein, that certain things which we all know are not statable, is in fact correct. Even notions as fundamental as truth, number and proper name cannot really be elucidated in any interesting way. In this very restricted respect, therefore, the notion of the "mystical" or something closely akin to it, intrudes on our quite ordinary thinking.

In general, the thesis that I've been arguing for in the last two chapters is that there are many concepts which are commonly employed but which are nonetheless ineffable in two closely related senses. First of all, although their meaning is perfectly clear, their meaning cannot be explicitly spelled out in an informative way. (The opposite *appears* to be the case and I tried to explain why this illusion arises.) Secondly, what these concepts refer to, or, the distinctions between types of things which these concepts demarcate, are definitely real, although, again, it is actually impossible to formally explain them. The *point* of this argument for our purposes here is that a very common and fairly obvious criticism of mysticism, that the language expressive of mystical beliefs is ineffable, amounts to saying that it is unintelligible; the mystic is not really saying anything although he may honestly believe that he is[3]. But if the argument of the last two chapters is correct, then this criticism is wrong and the situation more complex than such a critic allows for; there are perfectly acceptable concepts which work in a way analogous to the mystical ones. Furthermore, there are degrees of ineffability, a topic which will be discussed in the chapter on analogical meaning.

Before giving an example of this sort of criticism it will be useful to consider a somewhat different and very interesting argument, due to Paul Henle,[4] for the same conclusion arrived at here. He asks us to consider a "primitive" language for mathematics (call it PM) in which, for example, addition but not *commutation* can be expressed. (Commutation is the rule given by, e.g., a + b = b + a where a and b are variables ranging over numbers.) Where $\triangle$ and $\square$ are symbols for numbers, whereas we would write $\square + \triangle = \square + \triangle$ the users of PM write:

(a) $\quad \overset{+}{\boxed{\triangle}} = \overset{+}{\boxed{\triangle}}$

which is true but stands for

both $\quad \square + \triangle = \square + \triangle$ and $\square + \triangle = \triangle + \square$

Hence, there is no way of expressing commutation in PM *and a person who did understand it could not express his thought* unless he invented a new language. Hence, relative to PM, commutation is an ineffable concept.

Another law which would not be expressible in PM would be b - a = a - b since subtraction is expressed (we assume) by

(b) $\quad \overline{\square} = \overline{\square}$

A very interesting feature of the situation, as Henle points out is that a person who *did* understand that b - a ≠ a - b might attempt to express his belief by writing that *sometimes*

(c) $\quad \overline{\square} \neq \overline{\square}$

But *(c) taken literally*, as opposed to what our progressive mathematician intends, *is contradictory*. Similarly he might attempt to express commutation by repeating (a) which is rather like asserting a tautology. On the other hand the mathematician might be able to hint (so to speak) at what he was trying to express by means of metaphor or analogical language. It is also important to note that the mathematician in question would not be able to *explain* why he could not express his (true) thoughts except to say that he did not possess an adequate symbolism. We do, and *in this respect* the situation is different from that of the mystic, who might claim that no (human) language could express his thoughts. But I think that the situations are sufficiently analogous that Henle's argument (and those of the last two chapters) constitute a *partial* reply to the claim that William Alston makes at the end of a paper critical of the idea of ineffability. He says,

"To label something ineffable in an unqualified way is to shirk the job of making explicit the ways in which it *can* be talked about; just as to unqualifiedly label an expression (which is actually used) meaningless is to shirk the job of making explicit the sort of meaning it *does* have in these uses. There may be something in the world which can't be talked about in any way, but if so we can only signalize the fact by leaving it unrecorded."[5]

We cannot (as in the case of our progressive mathematician) stand outside the conceptual scheme of the mystic, examine the objects of his experience and then provide him with a more adequate language to express himself in. However, I agree with Alston that something more should be said and I will try to do this in the chapter on analogical meaning.

One last point, made by Richard Gale should be mentioned in this connection. I have been talking mostly about concepts. Gale points out that mystical experiences themselves are also not unique in being very difficult to describe. The same could be said of listening to Bach, seeing St. Mark's Square for the first time or, simply, seeing yellow. And probably the chief feature which such experiences have, to some, extent, in common with mystical ones is their *unique value* which is almost (perhaps entirely) impossible to convey in words.[6]

Notes to Chapter Three

1. See the first few pages of Frege's paper "Thoughts." There is an English translation of this paper in Gottlob Frege, *Logical Investigations*, ed., P. T. Geach, trans., P. T. Geach and R. H. Stoothoff (Oxford: Blackwell, 1977), pp. 1-30.

2. On this point see R. L. Goodstein's valuable paper "The Significance of Incompleteness Theorems" in his book, *Essays in the Philosophy of Mathematics* (Leicester University Press, 1965), pp. 153-166.

3. William Alston, "Ineffability," *The Philosophical Review*, 65 (1956). Reprinted in Steven M. Cahn, ed., *Philosophy of Religion* (New York: Harper & Row, 1970), pp. 283-300.

4. Paul Henle, "Mysticism and Semantics" in Cahn, pp. 274-282.

5. Alston, p. 300.

6. Richard M. Gale, "Mysticism and Philosophy", in Cahn, pp. 301-314.

CHAPTER FOUR

Analogical Meaning in Theology

At the end of Chapter III, I alluded to the claim that not all theological assertions are on a par, although the vast majority are certainly not straightforward empirical propositions and certainly *no* mystical claims fit into the latter category. Some religious statements are not, however, ineffable *tout court* and are not "literal" either, but rather fall into a third category. Their meaning is *analogical.* What I intend to do in this chapter is to try to explain how the question of analogical meaning is itself *analogical,* i.e., to explain how the question of analogical meaning arises and defend the view that there really is this sort of meaning. I will approach this topic by discussing some of the views of St. Thomas Aquinas.

Aquinas argues in the first part of the *Summa Theologica* that specifically religious doctrines (as opposed, for example, to historical claims which are relevant to religion) are often not provable except in the sense that sometimes one dogma may be deducible from others, e.g., if one accepts the authority of the Bible then certain other things will of course follow. (For Aquinas, of course, the dogmas of religion are those of the Roman Catholic Faith but the same philosophical points could apply to other religious beliefs.) There is however, a third category. These are doctrines which can be proven using natural human reason. (They can also be believed by faith by those who do not accept the proofs or are unaware of the proofs or cannot follow them.) Examples of these sorts of doctrines are the immortality of the soul and the existence of God. I will not discuss these proofs here except to point out that although they provide no information concerning the essential nature of God, they do appear to allow us to talk intelligibly about God as Cause and Sustainer of the world (the first three proofs), as perfectly good (fourth proof) and as Omniscient, or at least infinitely more intelligent that we are (fifth proof). But Aquinas also states that God in no way resembles creatures, i.e., resembles anything in the world with which we are normally familiar (*Summa* 1a, Q4, Art. 3). Hence, the above claims cannot derive their meaning from a *similarity* between (for example) God as Creator and an artist. Furthermore, St. Thomas explicitly *denies* that such a proposition as "God is wise" means no more than "God is the cause of human wisdom," as one might wrongly surmise from Aquinas first two proofs (*Summa* la, Q13, Art. 2).

The question naturally arises, therefore, as to how theological statements are meaningful at all since, on Aquinas' own account, such things as 'wise' or 'loving' or 'powerful' do not have their usual meaning in application to God, nor can their meaning be explained in the above mentioned ways. Aquinas' short answer to this question about meaning is that theological assertions are *analogical*. There are four questions concerning this. (1) What does Aquinas mean? (2) Is analogical usage in general defensible or is it just a kind of equivocation; so that we really don't know *what* theological statements mean? (3) Can there be a *theory* of analogy? (4) How is analogy to be applied theologically? To answer these questions we need to consider the different *types* of analogy traditionally distinguished.

"Analogy of proportionality" is understood in importantly different senses by different authors, and it is not always entirely clear what problem the analogy is designed to solve or how it would solve it. The clearest interpretation of the analogy of proportionality appears to be its construal as exactly like the following simple mathematical case: x is to a as b is to c; a, b and c are knowns, x is not; solve for x. This is then applied to problems of meaning in religious contexts through its apparent exact analogy with (for example) God's wisdom (x) is to God (a) as a man's wisdom (b) is to man (c): solve for "God's wisdom." But as Geach[1] and others have remarked, this is of no use at all for here *a* is an unknown also (or, at least, as unknown as x). (Another sense of proportionality is considered later.) Proportionality is often contrasted with analogy of attribution or proportion and with analogy of inequality. The first (textual) question then is how Aquinas intended his various classifications of analogy to be understood. This question overlaps with two others: what sort of analogy did St. Thomas think was theologically important and what sorts of relations are there between the various types of analogy?

One view is that there is a development in St. Thomas's views about analogy. In his early works he favors analogy of proportionality as the most useful in theological contexts and in his later works, analogy of attribution.[2] But this seems to be correct only in the following respect: that Aquinas allows a sense of "analogy of proportionality" (not the above one) which has some application in religious discourse, but this sort of analogy of proportionality appears to be really just a species of analogy of attribution and, further, depends on the prior applicability of attribution to give it a sense. (In some non-religious contexts the last conditions need not be met.) This constitutes a schematic answer to the first two questions above. In the course of trying to justify this answer I hope to provide an answer to the third question.

In the early *Commentary on the Sentences of Peter Lombard* Thomas distinguishes[3] three sorts of analogy; (1) According to intention and not according to being for which he gives his stock example of "health" as applied to animals (properly), to urine (a certain kind being an effect of health), and to diet (a certain kind being a cause of health). The label here seems confusing: what must be meant, I think, is that there is no analogy "according to being" but an actual (causal) relationship whereas the term is being used analogically. (2) Analogy according to being but not intention: here the analogous term is used as if there were some property which the entities referred to had in common but actually there is none (or, at least, if there is a common property, it is not what is meant by the term). St. Thomas gives the antique example of "body" as applied to corruptible and incorruptible bodies, but "existent," "beautiful," "good," "thing," and "number" would be acceptable examples. There is a *ratio* for the application of "existent" to a fleeting mental image and to a stone, but the explanation is not that there is a mysterious property, existence, shared by both. (3) According to intention and being: "this is when they are equally matched neither in a common intention [meaning] nor in being ... I maintain that truth and goodness and the like are predicated analogically of God and creatures. This means that according to their being [*esse*] all these exist in God and in creatures according to their greater or lesser perfection." Given that St. Thomas does not allow a gradation of value but rather stresses the unlimited gap between God and creation,[4] the last phrase must just mean (in part) according to what properties they have. Given that "to be" is "to be _____" where the blank is filled in with a general term[5] this is clear from Thomas's next remark, "From this it follows that since they cannot exist according to the same being in both, they are diverse truths," i.e., they fall under different concepts although the same word is applied analogously to them.

There are three points worth noticing about these texts: (1) none mention analogy of proportionality (in the mathematical sense mentioned above); I will leave Cajetan's sense for the moment); (2) they suggest that the "theory" of analogy is both logical and ontological (or, at the very least, a theory about words based on considerations about the nature of reality); (3) all three sorts seem to have application in theological discourse: for example, the first in talking of God as Creator and Sustainer of the world; the second in saying that God exists; and the last in speaking of God as wise or benevolent. I conclude thus far that St. Thomas is mainly concerned to discuss types of analogy of attribution (rather than to contrast this with other types) and that this is the sort of analogy he thinks is theologically relevant.[6] This is confirmed by what St. Thomas says in the *Summa*, I, q.13, a.5 where he distinguishes only two sorts of analogy, "of many to one" (*multorum ad unum*) which corresponds to the first sort mentioned in the Commentary on the Sentences, and "one to many" (*unius ad alterum*) which roughly corresponds to the second two sorts in the Commentary. Both are clearly analogies of attribution (or proportion).

At this point it is useful to consider a slightly different interpretation suggested by James F. Ross in his valuable paper, "Analogy As a Rule of Meaning for Religious Language."[7] After quoting Aquinas on analogy of attribution (*I Contra Gentiles ch.34*) Ross says, "This argument is useful only if enough similarity has already been demonstrated between God and other things to justify a statement that a causal relation holds. ... Even if there is such an analogy, it cannot be the basic one, for it supposes true statements about God."[8] This seems to me an extraordinary remark. Of course, the analogy does presuppose "true statements about God," but according to Aquinas we have such statements by means of the Five Ways (the term commonly used for St. Thomas' five proofs for The existence of God) or through Revelation. In any case, there can clearly be no question of analogy of any sort without some statements the meaningfulness of which we are attempting to explain. Ross might seem to be correct here on the grounds that it does not appear coherent to hold both that a certain statement, e.g., "God exists" is true, and yet there is some doubt as to its meaningfulness. This describes the situation incorrectly; rather we have a statement known (or believed) to be both true and meaningful, and then a question arises as to how its meaning is to be explained.   If an explicit understanding of a philosophically adequate theory of meaning were a necessary condition of using a language at all, we would be in the position of not being able to speak. Ross' own view appears to be that terms applying to God initially get their sense by means of analogy of proportionality[9] e.g., an acceptance of Aquinas' first argument for the existence of God enables us to say that God "moves" the world; an acceptance of the third that he "conserves" the world. These can then be translated into "names" of God which apply to him by analogy of attribution; from "He causes the world" to "causer," from "He conserves the world" to "conserver." Ross is here using the expression "analogy of proportionality" in a different sense from that criticized by Geach; he simply means it to cover cases where we have a similarity of relations rather than of one-place predicates.[10] Without intending to indulge in semantics in the bad sense this would seem to make analogy of proportionality a kind of analogy of attribution; this at any rate seems to be closer to Aquinas' own mind on the matter. But there are difficulties with Ross' view. How, for instance, can "wise" or "omnipotent" be applied to God through transference from a relation? One possibility, that "God is wise" means no more than "God is the cause of wisdom" is explicitly denied by Aquinas [11] (though it may be correct that the latter statement gives us an initial hint as to the meaning of "God is wise"). Another possibility of explaining these terms relationally stems from Aquinas' fourth argument for God's existence. Since this purports to establish that God is the exemplar of wisdom, goodness, and the like, it might be construed as providing the basis of meaningful predications concerning

God through analogy of proportionality in Ross' sense (and not analogy of attribution) by reason of our understanding of the ordinary usage of "wisdom" and "good" and of the relational expression "being paradigmatic with respect to." This would at least have the advantage of not being open to Geach's objection to analogy of proportionality, for in this case we would have three knowns (wisdom or goodness, creatures, and the relation *is paradigmatic relative to*) and one unknown (God): we would not be simultaneously trying to solve for the relation and one of its *relata*. But this clearly will not work either because one could not possibly understand the application of the relevant relational term without at least tacitly understanding that the first relatiom is a paradigm, i.e., without understanding something by the application of "wise" or "good" to God, i.e., the meaning of "x is a paradigm with respect to ... " depends on the meaning of 'x'. Hence, again, it is analogy of attribution which is fundamental,[12] though we certainly have analogy of proportionality (in Ross' sense) as well, as when it is said that God's causing the world is somehow analogous to a composer's creation of a piece of music without the aid of any pre-existent material. In short, we will have analogy with respect to a relational or non-relational term depending on which sort of predication we are attempting to make.

The answer to the scholarly question of what sort of analogy St. Thomas meant to have application in religious contexts is then, simply, all sorts depending on the type of predicate being applied to God, with the proviso that analogy of proportionality in the mathematical sense has no application at all. (As St. Thomas hints, no classification of types of analogy of attribution can be complete unless the classification is a purely formal one. This is discussed below.)

All this naturally suggests the question of whether we really need analogous terms at all or whether analogy is just an unnecessary species of equivocation. This is easily confused with a quite different question, viz., is it possible to construct some general theory which will explain the mechanism of analogous predication?

With regard to the first question, clearly some analogous usages can be dispensed with, e.g., we could always speak of "types of food which are productive of health" rather than "healthy" foods. But, as I shall try to show by means of examples, there are all sorts of analogous uses of terms which are perfectly meaningful and are not reducible to nonanalogous uses, i.e., to univocal or equivocal terms which have their meaning in virtue of some property common to the entities to which the terms apply. (Color words and expressions describing the dimensions of things seem to be obvious examples of such univocal usages.) Wittgenstein has already shown that there are many unambiguous meaningful terms which are not univocal in this sense. (These would be called "analogical" by Aquinas according to the account quoted at the beginning of this chapter.) Two of Wittgenstein's examples are "game" and "understanding"; there is, for instance, no single criterion such as the presence of a certain internal "mental state" for the application of "understanding."[13] Here are some further examples. As Aristotle argued at length, "pleasure" is not the name of a single sensation or other mental state which is present whenever a person is enjoying himself: drinking whiskey and listening to Bach are both pleasurable but not through the existence of a single "property" of both types of experience. Pleasure is defined in terms of its object, and these objects do not fall under a single concept except "pleasurable." Nonetheless, there is nothing obscurantist in the ordinary application of the word to these very various things and, in fact, this usage could not be dispensed with. Hence the usage of "pleasure" is both analogical and unavoidable. Similarly, consider "perceives" in application to, e.g., humans, dogs, and amoeba. We certainly have grounds for applying the term to all three, but in application to amoebas it seems to be an analogical extension; similarly with "loyal" as applied to dogs. A different kind of example is the use of "resolution" by psychoanalysts: this obviously has important connections with its lay usages in application to the solving of purely intellectual problems. A last example I will mention is "implication." This has both analogical and equivocal uses. In application to propositions which state logical or causal connections and to those which express conditional intentions it is analogical. It might be said to have a "root meaning" that is expressed by the material implication of truth functional logic but, although this is certainly common to all its usages, it is not the meaning of any of them.

Such examples might be claimed to arise from the (alleged) "imprecision" of ordinary speech, but I think such a criticism would be mistaken. "Pleasure" as used by a psychologist or "matter" by the physicist have different meanings from the same terms as ordinarily used, but these meanings have important connections and we could not simply drop the one usage in favor of the other: what we do say, rather, is that the physicist has a more profound understanding of matter (ordinary usage) than the layman does. Also analogical usages occur within the sciences (e.g., "number" in application to natural, negative, transfinite, and ordinal numbers[14]).

These examples illustrate, I think, the important slogan that analogy is itself analogous, i.e., there is no one second-order property or set of properties that all these analogous usages have in common. Hence, the misguided attempt to delineate such a property is apt to leave the impression that the doctrine of analogy is just a bit of specious obscurantism.

With this in mind I would like to comment briefly on the idea of a theory of analogy. As I hope the previous examples show, that there is correct analogous usage is just a fact about language. This fact is sometimes denied, I think, through approaching language with a preconceived and mistaken idea of how analogous usage must function if it is really to be intelligible. This can be illustrated by some remarks of J. J. Heaney[15] made in an article criticized by J. F. Ross.[16] Concerning Bochenski's example[17] of "sees" in "John sees a cow here" and "John sees the truth of the first theorem of Goedel" Heaney says, "First of all, the argument [sic] for ... these two expressions being analogous ... relies on the rather tenuous assumption that 'seeing' a cow and 'seeing' something which is 'the truth' of a theorem must be construed as sharing something in addition to being spelled the same way. In actual use, however, this is not the case: physiological and intellectual 'seeing' are in fact never confused with each other." Following Ross it seems obvious to me that these two uses of "see" are analogous (though I would agree with Heaney to this extent, that the analogy is a rather extended one). Why should anyone deny this? I think in this case it is simply due to a deep prejudice about language which Wittgenstein has exposed, viz., the idea that if a term applies unambiguously in two contexts then there must be some specifiable property (or set of properties) "referred to" by the term in the two cases and which either is the meaning of the term or that in virtue of which the term has the meaning it has. If one operates on this erroneous assumption then, of course, one will come to the conclusion that the use of a term which is in fact analogous is equivocal, since one will be unable to discover the single relevant property. That Heaney has made this mistake comes out in his insistence that the two uses of "see" must share something if the term is to be unequivocal, and in his remark that the second use of "see" does not have as part of its meaning "the physical ability to see" - of course it does not since the two uses are (only) analogous. The only reason there could be for Heaney making this remark at all would have to be based on the mistaken presupposition that either the two uses have this in common or the term is ambiguous.

It might be objected that, after all, I have not presented any theory of analogy (even less of meaning in general) which shows that Heaney's contention is incorrect; I've simply suggested that it is based on an erroneous assumption about language and appealed to our "intuitions" about the meaningfulness of terms (not intuitions in any metaphysical sense but rather beliefs based on our observation of how the language we use actually works). This is correct, though I think real examples do show that the relevant assumption is only a prejudice. I will now attempt some brief comments on the idea of a theory of analogy.

The view I wish to defend is, quite bluntly, that one type of theory of analogy is impossible and that attempts to construct theories of this sort are based on the erroneous presuppositions discussed above. The type of theory I mean is the sort where an attempt is made to delineate some set of properties which all analogous usages have in common. Given that analogy is itself analogous, such an enterprise is bound to fail. Even Bochenski's very valuable contribution to this problem seems to suffer to some extent from this assumption, for his fundamental idea appears to be that if two relational terms are analogous they must have the same formal properties. This may be a correct and important point about analogy but it is equally important to note[18] that (1) the formal properties of the analogous terms cannot be construed as the meaning of those terms; and, (2) having identical formal properties may be a necessary condition of two terms (strictly, two usages of the same term) being analogous but it is certainly not a sufficient condition (e.g., "larger than" and "is more spiritual than" have the same formal properties but they do not appear to be analogous in any interesting sense). Thus (as I think Bochenski would allow), although this formal analysis throws a good deal of light on the problem of analogy, it does not constitute a theoretical explanation of it.

Another example is this. Following Bochenski and others one might be tempted to explain analogy in terms of a "continuum of meaning." The latter phrase is ambiguous but one account of it is the following. For our purposes here let us suppose that the identity relation is relative.[19] This really comprises two theses which have been called by Wiggins[20] the D-thesis, viz., that if two "things" are identical with respect to some general substantial concept (like "gold" or "sodium"); "a = b" must mean "a f· b" where f is an abbreviation for some concepts and the R-thesis (relativity thesis) that $\underline{a}$ may be identical with $\underline{b}$ relative to one concept and not relative to another. Let us allow that both these theses are true (Wiggins himself argues only for the truth of the first). Let A1, A2 . . .An be second-order properties of terms (analogous and otherwise), f and f^1 stand for relational and non-relational terms. Then one of Bochenski's points could be put in this way: if "f $\underset{A_1}{=}$ f^1" is true then it must be true that "f $\underset{A_2}{=}$ f^1" and "f $\underset{A_3}{=}$ f^1, etc., are true where A1 and A2, etc., represent second-order formal properties. We might then be tempted to generalize this. In the case of pure univocation we have: (for all A) (f = f^1), i.e., the criteria for the application of f and f^1 (which would usually represent the same word) are exactly the same in all contexts. (The above code means: for all properties A, f and f^1 are identical relative to A.) In the case of less

than pure equivocation we have:

$$(EA)(f = f^1) \ \& \ (EA)(f = f^1)$$
$$\qquad A1 \qquad\qquad A2 \text{ etc.}$$

but we also have (EAn) (f = f^1),
$$\qquad An$$

(i.e., there exist properties relative to which f and f¹ are identical and there exists at least one property relative to which they are not identical). Then as we move further down the scale we have cases where the two usages have fewer and fewer second-order properties in common -- these are the analogous usages -- until we finally reach pure equivocation: i.e., there exists no property relative to which f and f¹ are identical;

in symbols, $\sim(EA)\ (f = f^1.)$

A

Even were this correct it would provide no precise way of distinguishing analogical from equivocal usages, but in any case it suffers from the above mentioned defect for it reduces to an attempt to explain "analogous similarity" in terms of an (higher-level) identity with respect to some property. And we have already seen that f and f¹ can be analogous without this similarity being explicable in terms of any identical property.

In general, given that analogy is analogous, it appears that any general theory of analogy is likely to fail since any account of the relevant similarity relation will be either too schematic (and thus not really explain anything) or fallaciously attempt to isolate some single property of the relation. The proper conclusion seems to be simply that analogy is *sui generis*.[21] (I hasten to add that this conclusion must necessarily be tentative since it is impossible to show that every type of explanation must fail.)

It is undoubtedly possible to give particular accounts of particular analogous usages (as Aquinas does of "healthy"), but it is difficult to see how one could ever give a complete list of types of analogy, although this does not seem to be precluded in principle, as is a general account in terms of a single set of properties.

So far I hope to have established that (a) Aquinas held in effect that various types of analogy of attribution are the ones which have application in religious contexts, and that this position is correct (if analogy can be used at all in such contexts); (b) that in ordinary contexts analogical usage is acceptable and, indeed, unavoidable, but (c) there does not now exist, nor is it likely that there ever will exist some theory of meaning which will explain analogical usage. There remain some special problems about the use of analogical terms in theological contexts that I would like to briefly discuss. The standard general problem is that the remoteness of God makes it unclear as to whether the application of our terminology to God retains any content at all; more specifically, it is said, for example, that God is wise but in a different sense from that in which (say) Socrates is wise, so we seem to have a piece of equivocation. There is undoubtedly a certain (probably unavoidable) lack of clarity here since, as Aquinas says, we do not have any insight in this life into God's *esse* ("being"), but given that (b) and (c) above are correct we can at least make the following negative remark. Since there is no objection to analogical usage in general, the onus appears to be on the objector to show why this particular analogical extension is unacceptable (as one might explain why the term "neurotic" cannot even be applied analogically to an amoeba). Further, given (c), there can be no theoretical logically conclusive grounds for rejecting the intelligibility of theological language (as, for instance, the logical positivists' claimed). As an example consider "good." The descriptive content of good derives from the class of things to which the term is applied[22] (e.g., a good cat is sleek, friendly etc.; a good proof is original, perspicuous). Leaving aside for the moment that the fact that God is the Exemplar of goodness, it presumably follows that the word "good" in application to God gets its sense from God's nature. Of this as such we have no knowledge, but we have some knowledge of God's "actions" from Revelation, or, to a lesser extent, natural theology (for those who believe it yields any results) or, in some cases from personal religious experience.[23] This is, at least in part, what must give "good" its content. Such a content must of necessity be incomplete, but it need not be any more imprecise than the knowledge we can be said to have of a person some of whose actions we are familiar with but whom we do not know very well. This gives the appearance of a "meaning gap"[24] which can be bridged only by believers, a notion which is not obviously intelligible: how, for instance, can a person try to believe what he can only understand if he believes. I think it is just partly true and partly false that there is such a gap, and I shall not try to elaborate on this as D. Z. Phillips has already done so,[25] except to point out that the unbeliever can sensibly be said to understand what it is (in part) that the believer believes in order to give his analogical predications substance, without himself believing those things.

There is a second, more difficult problem about analogical predication in religion. This stems from the fact that God is said to be the paradigm of goodness, wisdom, truth, etc. From this it would appear that the primary sense of such terms is given in their application to God (as Aquinas says) and that their application to temporal things is somehow derivative. This is paradoxical to say the least: since we have no knowledge of God's nature, to say that the paradigm of the use of "good" is in application to God appears to be the worst sort of metaphysical mumbo jumbo. But this problem is not insurmountable. There are perfectly ordinary cases where we learn to correctly use analogous terms without realizing that there even is a primary application of the term (e.g., good as used in non-theological contexts). Consider for example "proof." One may begin by using this term (correctly) in application to very imprecise examples, then (say) in application to simple truth-functional examples, to mathematical ones, to metalogical ones, and finally realize that there is no clearly specifiable limit to how "good" a proof can be.[26] We thus understand a hierarchy of perfection with respect to proofs and the idea of a paradigm without any exact idea of what the paradigm would be like (I do not mean that *here* we are forced to say that a paradigm exists); so, again, there does not seem to be grounds for a general, theoretical objection to such an idea being used in theological contexts.

Notes to Chapter Four

1.   P. T. Geach and G. E. M. Anscombe, *Three Philosophers* (Oxford: Blackwell's, 1963), p. 123.

2.   H. A. Wolfson, "St. Thomas on Divine Attributes," (reference in Julius R. Weinberg, *A Short History of Medieval Philosophy*: Princeton, 1964).

3.   First part of *Commentary on the Sentences*.

4.   See, for instance, *Summa Theologiae*, I, q.4, a.3: "Although we may admit in a way that creatures resemble God we may in no way admit that God resembles creatures. (Ad quartum dicendum quod licet aliquo modo concedatur quod creatura est similis Deo mullo tamen modo concedendum est quod Deus sit similis Creaturae.)"

5.   In this I am following Geach's analysis of *esse*. It is not to deny either the distinction between a thing's *esse* and its being a such and such, nor the identification of God with his *Esse*.

6.   I take it that Robert E. Meagher has successfully shown that Cajetan (in his *De nominum analogia*) was mistaken in his inter-pretation of St. Thomas on this point. See Meagher, pp. 230-253.

7.   In A. Kenny, ed., *Aquinas: A Collection of Critical Essays* (Macmillan, 1969), pp. 93-138.

8.   Ibid., p. 110, footnote 13.

9.   Ibid., pp. 135-137.

10. Ibid., p. 129.

11. *Summa Theol.*, I, q. 13, a. 2.

12. Ross seems to reverse his position to one like this when he says ". . . these terms wisdom, simplicity and the like in application to God can all be turned into 'relation predicates'. ... " (Ibid., pp. 136-137).

13. L. Wittgenstein, *Philosophical Investigations*, Part I, Sections 66-69 and 138-155. I owe this idea that Wittgenstein's philosophy could be an aid in understanding Aquinas to Anthony Kenny's very interesting paper "Aquinas and Wittgenstein," *The Downside Review* (Summer-Autumn, 1959), pp. 217-235.

14. The example is Wittgenstein's.

15. J.J. Heaney, "Analogy and "Kinds" of Things," *The Thomist* XXXXV, no. 2 (April, 1971), pp. 293-304.

16. J. F. Ross, "A Response to Mr. Heaney," ibid., pp. 305-311.

17. I. M. Bochenski, "On Analogy," Albert Meen, ed., *Logico-Philosophical Studies* (Dordecht-Holland: D. Reidel, 1962), pp. 97-117.

18. This is in no sense intended as a criticism of Bochenski's work but only of certain ideas which it might erroneously be thought to entail.

19. P. T. Geach has argued for this position in his paper "Identity," *Review of Metaphysics* (September, 1967), Vol. XXI, pp. 3-12.

20. David Wiggins, *Identity and Spatio-Temporal Continuity* (Oxford: Basil Blackwell, 1967).

21. Cf. one of John E. Thomas' conclusions in his paper, "On The Meaning of 'Analogy is Analogous.'" *Theologique et Philosophique*

(Laval), Vol. XXII, pp. 73-79. On p. 79 Professor Thomas says, ". . . clearly what stands in the way of specifying the meaning of 'analogy is analogous' is the failure to solve the problem of the *ratio communis* of analogous expression." If my own view is correct, there simply is no *ratio communis*.

22.   On this point see P. T. Geach, "Good and Evil," *Analysis*, vol. 17 (1956), pp. 33-42.

23.   Cf. Donald F. Duclow, "Pseudo-Dionysius, John Scotus Eriugena, Nicholas of Cusa: An Approach to the Hermeneutic of the Divine Names," *International Philosophical Quarterly*, Vol. XII, no. 2 (June, 1972), pp. 260-278.

24.   I owe this expression to Brian Calvert.

25.   D. Z. Phillips, "Religious Beliefs and Language Games," *Ratio*, 12 (1970), pp. 26-46.

26.   Cf. Iris Murdoch on the idea of perfection in *The Sovereignty of Good* (London: Routledge & Kegan Paul, 1970).

CHAPTER FIVE

The Ontological Argument for the Existence of God

This chapter is an attempt to defend a version of the ontological argument for the existence of God. The ontological argument strikes virtually everyone, on first hearing it, as obviously fallacious, although some version of it has been defended by a number of well known philosophers, e.g., St. Anselm, Descartes, Spinoza and Leibniz.

I will start off by giving a simplified version of the argument, discuss some standard objections to this version, and then consider some modern versions. The argument was first propounded by the 12th century Christian philosopher St. Anselm of Canterbury. St. Anselm starts out by saying that the concept of God, i.e., the concept with which he was familiar, the traditional Jewish and Christian concept, is the concept of that than which none greater can be conceived. Another way of saying the same thing would be to assert that the concept of God is the concept of that Being which possesses the traditional properties of omnipotence, omniscience and so on, but also a rather strange property of necessary existence which only God possesses. It is perhaps worth noting right off that the question of whether or not this is the correct concept of God appears to be irrelevant, since all that St. Anselm and others are arguing is that there is this particular idea of God and that on the basis of it the existence of God can be proven.

Now suppose that God exists only as a concept. In that case our concept is not really a concept of God, although it appears to be, because, first of all, we can conceive of a "greater," viz., a God that has extramental existence and, secondly, what is a mere concept does not exist necessarily. It then follows from this that, necessarily, St. Anselm's concept of God has to be the concept of something that actually exists. Traditionally it was thought that the argument applies only to God, since only He is thought of as enjoying underived necessary existence, but this feature of the argument may not be correct; I will return to this point later.

There are very obvious objections to this argument. One which was raised in St. Anselm's own day is that it appears that this kind of argument could be used to prove the existence of anything to which one assigned the "property" of necessary existence. I will have more to say about this objection later; for the moment we need to note simply that most non-mathematical objects are just not the sorts of things to which it makes sense to assign necessary existence. It is unintelligible, for example, to assert of a book or a planet that it is not possible that it does not exist, since obviously things of this sort can pass into and out of existence. A second very general objection is that there must be some sort of illicit passage in the argument from thought to reality, for it is impossible to prove the existence of any non-mathematical object without making some observation of the empirical world. As it stands, however, this objection seems to beg the question, for the point defenders of the ontological argument are making is that, oddly enough, in this one case, one *can* pass from thought to existence. A third objection that has been raised is that the idea of God is incoherent or contradictory in some respect and hence the conclusion cannot really be understood. This is related to the very subtle problem of how theologians can say on the one hand that God is ineffable yet still talk about Him. As we have seen, St. Thomas Aquinas argues that since we have no insight into God's essence in this life any predications which are made about him would have to be analogical only. As I have already tried to argue, this position is defensible, although it is unlikely that it is possible to *prove* that the notion of God is consistent. The fourth and most important objection which seems to have been understood by Aristotle and Aquinas and was explicitly stated in the modern period by Kant, is that existence is not an ordinary property on a par with other properties such as being red or being 10 meters long. This fact is brought out in the simple observation that the descriptions of real and unreal objects can be exactly the same. For example, if I give a thoroughgoing description of the cat in my room, I don't give you any further information about him by saying that he exists. I think in fact that this objection is quite effective against any version of the ontological argument, *if* there is any such version, which does presuppose that existence or necessary existence is an ordinary first-order property. However, the version I intend to defend here does not make this assumption. In modern logic, existence is not treated as an ordinary first-order concept but as a second-order concept about concepts, which states that the concept in question has instances. In the case of positive existential statements, for example, to say that there is a cat in my room is just to say that something falls under the concept - *a cat in this particular room*. And this is expressed in the notation of formal logic by having an existential quantifier as opposed to a term which designates the property of existence. Thus, to write the statement "There is a cat in my room" as "There exists an X such that X is a cat and X is in my room" is not the silly pedantry that it may appear to be, but in fact makes clear an important philosophical point. Thus, in order to avoid the standard criticism of the ontological argument, what we need to do is simply state the premises of the argument in such a way that the existential quantifier is employed instead of any assumption which would treat existence as an ordinary concept. Hence all we need to do is restate the proposition "If God exists at all then He has the property of existing necessarily," as "If God exists *at all* then *necessarily* there exists a being such that that being is God." In the simple formal proof given below its important to realize that the letter "p" is not a propositional variable which takes any proposition as value, but an *abbreviation* for a single proposition, the proposition "God exists." "L" will, as is usual in modal logic stand for "its necessary that" and "M" for "its possible that"; "~" means *not*, "->" stands for material implication (a minimal sense of "if...then") and "<>" is an abbreviation for material equivalence ("if and only if"). The first two premises are substantial (and controversial) theological ones; the third an obvious thesis of modal logic and the fourth a more controversial statement.

The version of the ontological argument presented here appears to be perfectly sound: the premises are true, or at least extremely plausible, quite independently of religious belief, and the steps are valid. I am disinclined, intuitively, as are most people, to believe that there can be a sound version of the Ontological Argument and came across this rendering in an attempt to refute one of Charles Harshorne's ingenious (and obscure) presentations of it.[1] The version presented here is inspired by his but appears to be importantly different. I will first of all state the argument unadorned and then discuss the justification for the premises and the way in which I believe this version of the argument avoids both the standard objections to it and the apparent ambiguity (in the use of the term "possible") in the famous interpretation due to Norman Malcolm. It is worthwhile repeating that it is *very* important to note that here "p" is understood as an abbreviation for a *particular* proposition, viz., the proposition that God exists; it is *not* intended as a propositional variable. The latter would render the argument vacuous in the following respect; if the first premise were generally true for a particular proposition (or set of propositions) as here claimed, then we could simply substitute '~p' for 'p' in premise 1 and easily show that p, Mp and Lp are equivalent. A modal logic containing such a thesis would, of course, be empty (since there must some real distinction between Lp and Mp for it to have a point). For our purposes here, essentially the same point can be put in this way: if the first premise were generally true any consistent existential statement would be true and so the argument presented here, though valid, would be circular. The letter "a" on the other hand is a variable taking propositions as value. "L," as usual, stands for the modal operator, it is logically necessary that, "M" for it is possible that, and the other symbols are standard logical ones.

1. $p \to Lp$ "Anselm's principle."

2. Mp An expression of the thesis that the concept of God is consistent.

3. $La \to a$ Obvious thesis of modal logic.

4. $\sim La \to L\sim La$

7.	~p -> L~p	Substitution in 4 using the equivalence established at 6.
8.	~L~p -> ~(~p)	Transposition in 7
9.	Mp <-> p	Standard modal equivalence Mp <-> ~L~p and double negation on 8.
10.	p	2, 9 Modus Ponens.

With regard to the concept of existence, what we need to notice for purposes of the above argument is that, in the assertion "God exists," "exists" is used simply in the sense of modern logic, i.e., "p" is to be understood as an abbreviation for the proposition "(Ex)Gx" where G is short-form for whatever analogical predicates are thought to be true of the Diety. Hence, it is not here assumed that "existence" is a predicate in any controversial sense.

The first question that arises is whether or not each step in the argument must be provable, or a necessary truth, in order for the argument as a whole to be sound. Steps 5 through 10 present no problem in this regard since they follow from steps 1 through 4 and by standard rules of ordinary and modal logic; therefore, the question of necessary truth and provability only arises for steps 1 through 4. It seems that these must be necessary truths if the conclusion is consistent for the following reason. Suppose the main premises of the argument are each shown to be contingently true, then the conclusion of the argument, that is the proposition p, is also only contingently true. Let this sort of contingency be represented by M, then it must be the case that Mp implies M~p, that is, by the ordinary rules of modal logic, it is not necessary that p, which obviously conflicts with the first premise that p implies necessarily p and we have a straightforward contradiction. Hence, the question is, how would one show that premise 1, p implies necessarily p, and premise 2, it is possible that p, are themselves necessary truths?

One possibility with regard to the first premise is the following. According to the religious traditions with which we are here concerned, it seems to be true that if God exists at all he must exist in every possible world. According to the standard semantics for modal logic, it would immediately follow from this that the proposition that God exists, if it is true at all, is a necessary truth and the first premise would be established. This thesis depends however, for its intelligibility on some very complicated questions about the exact status of the idea of a possible world. If we treat a possible world as just any possible configuration and variation of the objects in this world,[5] then the thesis that God exists in every possible world if he exists at all follows very simply, but appears to have no significance. Hence the first premise is true "by definition" and in that sense is necessarily true. This might make the whole argument seem trivial, question-begging or both but this is not the case. The idea (in general) is just that a certain conception can render a certain conditional (not categorical) statement true. Hence, the first premise is just like such remarks as "If centaurs existed at all they would be found in Greece."

What the fourth premise asserts is that if a statement is not a necessary truth then this fact is itself a necessary truth. By a "necessary truth" I mean very generally (and in accordance with standard logical usage) a truth such that it is not possible for it not to be the case. Precisely what set of propositions (if any) fall into this category is a matter of some controversy, but most people would agree that mathematical theorems are a clear example. They are not, however, necessary *tout court* or necessary truths *about* the physical world, but rather, necessary (provable) *conditional* statements or axioms within certain systems. A famous example is the thesis that parallel lines never meet: this is an axiom (and therefore, trivially, a theorem) of Euclidean geometry but it is false in Riemannian geometry. Any theorem in Euclidean geometry which depends on this axiom is a "necessary truth" *in* Euclidean geometry (but not generally) or, which amounts to the same thing, the relevant *conditional* statement that if the relevant axioms are true the theorem in question is true is a necessary truth if we accept the rules of inference involved. The latter can be expressed as statements in which case they are probably the simplest examples of necessary truths, e.g., the simple rule of *modus ponens* can be expressed in this way: "If the statement p implies q and p is true, then so is q." Another class of examples are statements which are true in virtue of the meanings of the (non-logical) words in them. The example often given is, "All bachelors are unmarried." This assertion is obviously trivial as are most examples of this kind, but it is sometimes *very* important to recognize that the statements one is making are "analytic" or necessary in this respect (if they are). Necessary statements are to be contrasted with contingent ones such as "All bachelors are lonely," the truth-value of which clearly depends on the facts, or, "The geometry of physical space-time is Riemannian." The issue here is whether a metalogical statement (a statement *about* the logic of statements), viz., the assertion that such and such a proposition is contingent, is *itself* a necessary truth. This is what the fourth premise of our reconstruction of the ontological argument asserts. Now it would seem to me that providing that "*a*" in premise 4 is understood as a variable ranging over *propositions* (i.e., what is expressed by the sentences of a natural language), 4 is obviously true. The only thing that might make it *appear* false is that one and the same string of words in a natural language may in one set of circumstances express a mere tautology (a trivial necessary truth) and in other circumstances a contingent statement. The sentence, for example, "The sum of the internal angles of a triangle is 180 degrees" is a necessary truth within Euclidean geometry and a contingent statement (probably a false one) if treated as descriptive of the empirical world. It is also a contingent fact as to which proposition is being expressed by the sentence, and this might make it appear that the version of Becker's principle which constitutes premise 4 is false. But this is not the case since, once it is established *which* proposition is being expressed, *that* the proposition is or is not a necessary truth is itself a second-order necessary truth. This much seems clear and is all we need for our purposes here, although I admit that I cannot give a precise explication of just what sort of necessity is involved.

The second premise simply amounts to the assertion that the traditional concept of God is logically consistent, and an advocate of this version of the ontological argument might simply point out that if it's impossible, as in fact is the case, to prove even the consistency of recursive arithmetic, then surely the possibility of proving the consistency of a set of theological propositions is even more unlikely. There is certainly something in this criticism, but in a vague and extended sense of "provability" it may in fact be not particularly difficult to prove that the notion of God is consistent. What I mean is the following. A commonly accepted criterion of consistency for a formal system, first proposed by Post, is that a system S is consistent if it can be proven that there is some thesis of the system which is not provable; this on the grounds that if a system is inconsistent then every thesis of the system is provable.   Hence a theologian could prove that his notion of God is consistent in the following, rather logically primitive, fashion. He simply provides us with a list of those propositions, analogical or otherwise, which he takes to be true, but for our purposes here their sources are irrelevant and they can be based simply on some accepted Revelation. It would, of course, be impossible to prove that, in general, the list is complete, but it does not seem to be out of the question to claim that it is complete relative to some purpose or other. It would then be possible to prove that at least within this admittedly narrow theological "system" there existed some proposition concerning the Diety which it was impossible to prove.   It would then follow by Post's criterion that the relevant notion of God was consistent, providing, at least, that every true thesis of the "system" was either an axiom or a theorem. This would be easy to show since it could contain a finite number of statements. So far as the second premise of the above version of the ontological argument is concerned, the main point, I think, is really this: the assumption that the idea of God is consistent is presumably much weaker than the assumption that God exists and to that extent the above argument has a point.

There is a more arcane but logically secure way of looking at this matter from the point of view of mysticism. As was mentioned in Chapter One, all mystics claim that the ultimate object of their devotion and insight, God, the God-head, Brahman, the Tao, is ineffable in at least this respect, that no positive attributes can really be ascribed to

Him. There is an, in some ways virtually empty, exception to this in that the object of mystical devotion is often referred to as eternal Being as such, or the One, or in modern times, by the existentialist theologian Paul Tillich, as the "ground of being." One way of interpreting this doctrine would be to say that the only positive "attribute" which can be correctly and literally applied to God is that of existing necessarily. This need not be taken in the logically confused sense of claiming necessary existence to be a property on the same logical level as other properties which a thing might have or fail to have, but can be interpreted as we have done in our first premise as the claim that if God exists at all then He does so necessarily. But the logically rather odd upshot of all this for purposes of defending the ontological argument is that we need to assign to God (again, *not* for the purpose of constructing the argument) a single quasi-property only, viz., necessary existence in the sense explained. Assuming then that the thesis expressed by our first premise is intelligible and consistent and expresses all that needs to be said in this context at least, then there is obviously no problem whatever concerning the consistency of the concept of God, since only a *single* (noncontradictory) property has been assigned to Him. Thus, the second premise becomes transparently true. (This does, however, obviously leave us with a rather difficult problem about what the expression "God" is supposed to mean.) This approach to the problem of consistency has the advantage of according very closely with traditional mystical views on the subject.

The problems with the remaining steps of the argument are less severe. Premise 3 would have to be a thesis of any logic whatever which claimed to be modal since all it says is that if something is necessarily true it is true. Steps 5 through 10 are completely uncontroversial, depending entirely on standard rules of classical and modal logic. The modal equivalence used at step nine is simply the thesis that if it is not necessary that not-p then it is possible that p, which is a thesis of any modal logic whatever. The conclusion is so odd that I presume most professional philosophers, and other people interested in this kind of thing, would claim that it is unintelligible. What it asserts is that, concerning any being whatever, if that being is such that if he exists at all he exists necessarily, then that being *does* have to exist. This is quite independent of the question of what properties He may or may not possess or which we may or may not claim to know that He possesses. Rather than being unintelligible, it seems to me that this conclusion is very restricted and corresponds fairly precisely to the traditional notion of God's ineffability, which all mystics claim to be the case. For this to make any sense we must assume that there is some distinction between ineffability and unintelligibility, but that will have to be the subject of another section. Here I would like to make only one other point. If this version of the ontological argument is sound, i.e., the premises of the argument are true and the argument is valid, then St. Anselm's critics were in a sense correct that the argument could be used to prove the existence of anything which, if it exists at all, exists necessarily. This is not really a criticism, but simply something which is in fact the case if the argument is sound. Hence, if someone could delineate some set of things of a non-theological nature, which if they exist, exist necessarily, then he could in fact prove their existence. So for example, although it is not relevant to our purposes here, if concepts are such that if they exist they exist necessarily, and perhaps extra-mentally, and similarly with such things as sets of numbers, then it is in fact true that if the ontological argument is sound then some version of platonism is sound, in the sense that concepts and mathematical objects must exist necessarily if they exist at all.

Addendum

A standard objection to Professor Norman Malcom's famous version of the ontological argument can be stated in this way. Malcolm assumes that '~(Ex)Gx -> ~M(Ex)Gx' on the grounds that if God does not exist it is not possible for Him to happen to come into existence *at some time*. But elsewhere in his argument he uses M in the sense of *logically* possible and in this sense the above assumption is false, for from the hypothesis that there is no God it does not follow that His existence is logically impossible. If this ambiguity is resolved by making the two senses of "possible" explicit, then Malcolm's argument no longer follows as he states it; whether a sound version could be constructed I do not know. The present version uses the term "possible" only in the sense of logically possible.

The argument we have being considering here is of astonishing simplicity, and I certainly do *not* claim that as a matter of scholarly historical fact it provides an exposition of St. Anselm's view of the matter. Nor would I claim that the argument is "deep" or even especially significant. But it does appear to be sound and this, I think, is of some interest generally and in relation to what some mystics say about their experiences.

Notes to Chapter Five

1. C. Hartshorne, "The Logic of the Ontological Argument," in W. Rowe and W. Wainwright, eds., *Philosophy of Religion* (Harcourt, Brace, Jovanovich, 1973), pp. 108-110

2. There is an interesting discussion of this in Peter Geach's essay on Aquinas in his and Elizabeth Anscombe's *Three Philosophers* (Oxford: Blackwell, 1961).

3. See, for instance, the papers by G. E. Moore and William P. Alston in Alvin Plantinga, ed., *The Ontological Argument* (Garden City, New York: Doubleday, 1965).

4. There is a further problem, also discussed by Geach, concerning the status of existence in the sense of Aquinas' *esse*, but we can safely ignore this here since our interpretation of the Ontological Argument requires the notion of existence only in the logician's sense. I suspect Geach is correct, however, that the argument that St. Anselm intends uses existence in the sense of *esse*, so that the argument of this paper is not a modern expression of St. Anselm's. But I will not attempt here to deal with the very complicated historical question of how St. Anselm's text is to be interpreted.

5. Rescher refers to these as "proximately" possible worlds in his *A Theory of Possibility* (University of Pittsburgh Press, 1975).

6. Norman Malcolm, "Anselm's Ontological Arguments," in his *Knowledge and Certainty*, (Englewood Cliffs, New Jersey: Cornell University Press 1963).

CHAPTER SIX

Space and Individuals

In a later section we shall see that the concept of time appears, in a complicated way, to be strictly contradictory (like the description of something as both round and not round in the same respect and at the same time).

Questions concerning the division of parts of reality into individual objects and their location, i.e., questions about space, appear to me to be much more obscure. I will therefore not try to argue in this section for the possibly straightforward thesis that space is unreal and that our division of reality into manageable particular objects is ultimately pragmatic and arbitrary, but for a related and admittedly more obscure view, viz., that it is logically (and metaphysically) impossible to disentangle "subjective" and "objective" elements in our descriptions of the world, i.e., there can be some, but very little, clarity concerning the question of what is objectively given and empirical and what our own minds contribute in our descriptions of, and understanding of, reality. These questions are metaphysical ones but I will approach them using the tools and some of results of contemporary "analytical" philosophy.

We ought first to briefly consider this very general methodological issue directly: to what extent can we determine what "the world" or "reality" is like independently of our perception and conception of it? Certainly we are all inclined to say that ordinary considerations and scientific theories (and marginally scientific theories like some psychological ones) *reflect reality* to the extent that they "work," i.e., to the extent that correct but falsifiable[1] predictions can be made on the basis of them. But no one has succeeded in delineating precisely what this *reflection* consists in (other than the "connexion with reality" already mentioned) and, which is more important for our purposes here, no-one has really succeeded in clarifying the question of to what extent the "reality" with which ordinary propositions and scientific theories are "connected" is our own creation, so that the fact that there is a connection is less surprising. As Wittgenstein[2] has (I believe) tactily argued (in both his early and later periods) it is impossible for us to stand apart from our own conceptional scheme(s), ways of perceiving and language-games and "see" their connection with the world. We can only explore from within.[3] In order, for example, to *describe* the relation (or rather, many complex relations) between language and the world, one must employ a language and thus one has not escaped one's own conceptual scheme.

There is an important distinction that needs to be observed here between perceiving and conceiving. Unexpressed perception is ineluctably private; I can know what you are perceiving and both of us can express this in a public language but neither of us can experience the other's perception and thus we cannot compare or contrast them either. If there are differences in people's private experiences they must, however, be *systematic* ones, since the inability to detect differences is publicly detectable, e.g., it is possible that my private experiences of red is the same as yours of green, etc., but if I perceive both red and green as the same colour then this, of course, can be publicly determined. An apparent example of a systematic difference would be the possibility of my experience of the colour spectrum being the exact inverse of yours. Conceiving also has a private aspect, of course, but it is essentially a public, social and, perhaps, "inter-subjective" phenomenon since the fundamental vehicle of concept formation and expression is language and language is, as a matter of logical necessity, primarily a public phenomenon. I do not mean that a concept can be said to be possessed by a person if and only if he can correctly use the corresponding term in a language, but only that the latter is sufficient (not a necessary) condition of the former and, perhaps more importantly, that it would be incoherent to maintain that some standard, non-exceptional set of concepts *could* only be grasped privately by a single individual. The latter thesis, which was first formulated and argued for in a precise and explicit manner by the later Wittgenstein,[4] is in a way a simple and almost obvious one once its truth is seen, but it has, I believe, very deep philosophical implications. Most of these need not concern us, nor will I attempt to argue for the thesis here since the literature on this topic is so vast (there are references at the end of this section). But we do need to notice two points. (1) Since concepts are essentially public, when I refer later to conceptional matters as "subjective" I do not mean subjective in the sense of private to and peculiar to some single human being, but rather, dependent on human thought (conscious or otherwise). (2) Another, very general and important thesis which I believe Wittgenstein is tactily arguing for in various places in his later writings[5] is that we cannot simply divide true propositions (including philosophical ones) into empirical and logical truths. Some *a priori* true generalizations (i.e., truths which are grammatical or even metaphysical rather than scientific or bluntly empirical) admit of exceptions, or have exceptions built into them. What must be the case is only that the exceptions are *necessarily exceptions*[6] and not standard examples, e.g., normally, to genuinely have an intention entails that something be actually done[7], but obviously this is not *always* the case. Given this, I think it is consistent with Wittgenstein's rejection of the coherence of the idea of a private language to hold that there can be utterances and classes of statements (though not whole languages in the ordinary sense) whose meaning are essentially private providing that we recognize that *statements of this sort are necessarily exceptions to the rule.* I will try later to explain the point of this and provide appropriate examples. To overlook this point is to fall into a kind of second-order "verificationism" about meaning, a view which I believe Wittgenstein would have rejected, at least if it were presented as a universal truth. It must be *possible* to decide the meaning of most propositions we use, but it is not possible to decide them all at once and a few (necessarily a small percentage) cannot be decided at all.

Returning to the methodological issue the point might be summarized, as certain commentators on Wittgenstein have pointed out, by saying that we can only explore our language(s) and conceptional schemes from within. The construction of metalanguages, though very useful in certain contexts, does not enable us to escape this conclusion for the reasons given in Chapters Two and Three: a metalanguage *reflects* rather than *explains* the structure which it is used to describe except in purely formal cases where the object-language only represents a tiny fragment of our conceptional scheme (as in formal metalogical studies). But the latter consideration in no way justifies the idea that the possibility of constructing metalanguages will enable us to magically stand back from our own situation and observe the relation(s) of our minds to reality. It therefore seems to be the case that certain metaphysical procedures, deep and useful as they are in certain respects, are fundamentally misconceived, for they presuppose that there is a method for determining in what way certain very general features of phenomena result from the imposition on reality of certain categories of the human mind. There are a few, perhaps relatively simple, cases where it is clear that the "reality" we perceive is partly or wholly produced by us, as in the case of colours, tastes or outright delusions. Similarly, one can partly "produce" a friendly atmosphere by not being hostile oneself, but such psychological examples don't appear to clarify philosophical issues. The general metaphysical problem of the relation between mind and reality seems, therefore, to be unsolvable. Hence, all I can try to do in this section is to provide hints partly based on current logical research as to how reality is partly constructed by us.

The first point to observe is a relatively simple but important one. It is that the cardinality of a domain is relative to the concepts employed in counting the members of it. By a "domain" is meant a set of "objects" (concrete or abstract) being considered for some purpose of other; the "cardinality" of a domain is the number of objects in it. This point is due to Frege and has been more recently discussed by Professor P. T. Geach.[8] Consider the domain consisting of a library in an otherwise empty park. The question, "How many physical objects are there in this domain?" is clearly unanswerable. We have to specify what sort of objects we have in mind, e.g., the cardinality of this domain relative to the concept *library* is one, relative to that of *book* it is several thousand, relative to that of *pages of a book* much greater, and so on. (The same situation seems to obtain in the case of more precisely delineated abstract objects, e.g., relative to the concept *natural number* the set of numbers from one to ten contains ten "objects" but relative to the concept of set or class it contains many more.) Now P. T. Geach in his book *Mental Acts* has argued very effectively for the view that concepts are not directly "abstracted" from experience, i.e., it is not the case (as common sense and many philosophers and psychologists seem to presuppose) that concepts are learned in the following way: we learn the idea of "redness" by observing a great many red objects and abstracting redness from their other properties; we learn the notion of "twoness" by observing a large number of couples and abstracting the "property" of twoness from the others we observe, and so on. Geach is particularly convincing in his argument that numerical properties cannot be abstracted. I cannot state Geach's arguments better than he himself can, so I will not attempt to reproduce them here. A summary of one feature of them is this: it is impossible to teach a person a concept by *pointing to* the relevant property and hoping he will get the right idea, for there is always a great many ways in which this performance could be interpreted and no guarantee whatever that he would eventually get the "right idea." This is difficult to argue for both convincingly and briefly, largely I believe for psychological reasons. We are all very strongly inclined to accept (wrongly if Geach is correct) a strictly empiricist view of concept-formation; I therefore simply refer the reader to Geach's writings and those of the later Wittgenstein. Geach's conclusion is that concepts are created, not abstracted.[9] But it then follows that the cardinality of a domain is also (in part at least) a human construct, not an "objective given." The metaphysical implications of this will be discussed later in this chapter.

Professor Geach has also argued[10] that the identity relation is relative. Identity is the notion represented by the identity sign in mathematics and elsewhere and apparently in such expressions as, "That is the same person as the one to whom you were speaking yesterday." (There may be important differences between the relations covered by the term "identity" and these differences may have received insufficient attention in the philosophical literature on the topic but we will here be concerned with what these relations have in common.) Traditionally, identity has been treated as strict or absolute, i.e., it was assumed that if "a = b" was true, its truth was independent of the concepts involved or, which amounts to the same thing, if such a statement was true it was true relative to every relevant concept. (I say "assumed" rather than "argued for" since the issue was not seriously discussed until quite recently.) The rules governing identity (which can be found in any standard text of formal logic) were very simple ones such as transitivity (if a = b and b = c, then a = c) and symmetry (if a = b, then b = a). Leibniz's Law, which states that if a = b, then every property of a is a property of b and vice-versa, was thought to essentially characterize the identity relation. (It should be noted that some logicians who defend the idea of relative identity nonetheless also accept some version of Leibniz's Law.) Those who argue, as Professor Geach has, that identity is relative claim that it is possible for "two" things *a* and *b* to be identical relative to one concept and not relative to another. (Leibniz's Law can be preserved providing that not every property of the objects concerned is a property relative to which they are identical.) We are here concerned with particular concepts within "our conceptual scheme" and not with the deeper question of the relativity of the properties of domains to conceptual schemes in general, a subject too vast for this work and to be avoided in any case for the reasons given above. Here are three examples of the relativity of identity over time. (I believe it can also hold at a time but this is more controversial and need not concern us here.) The one is commonplace, one mathematical and the other taken from physics. (1). Consider a human being, N, at age ten (at this stage we will call him "Nt10" for N at time 10) and at age 40 (Nt40). There is clearly a sense of person (something like, having such and such personality characteristics) such that Nt10 is not the same person as Nt40 although they are the same human being or organism. (2) Even in mathematics we can apparently say, for example, that 2 is the same number as 4 but not the same function. (3) The physicist Fritjof says the following;

> "The structure of a hadron [a type of subatomic particle]...is not understood as a definite arrangement of constituent parts, but is given by all sets of particles which may interact with one another to form the hadron under consideration. Thus a proton exists potentially as a neutron-pion pair, a kaon-lambda pair, and so on."[11]

Thus, it appears correct to say that in a certain respect a proton is the same hadron as a particular neutron-pion pair but it is obviously not the same proton, since the neutron-pion pair is not a proton at all. (If the conclusion of the next section, that time is unreal, is correct, then the above conclusion is even more evident and we need not concern ourselves at all with the distinction between identity at a time and over time.) I will not attempt to argue for the thesis of relative identity other than by simply giving the above examples since this has been ably done elsewhere. In any case the thesis, although startling in a way, is relatively easy to understand and defend. The complications arise, rather, in answering objections to the thesis and attempting to refute it's detractors' assumption.[12] I will simply provide, parenthetically, one example here. Professor Wiggins has argued that such examples as (1) above involve, among other things, a confusion about tenses. Nt40 is strictly identical with the person he *was* at t10; he simply has *now* certain characteristics he lacked then. Thus, Wiggins argues, we need not introduce anything as bizarre as relative identity but simply observe that time makes change noncontradictory. But this seems to me to simply evade the issue. It is true that Wiggins' account is faithful to how we ordinarily think about the matter, but it is simply not the case that if "Nt10 = Nt40" is to satisfy the ordinary criteria of strict identity they must have every property in common; Leibniz's Law simply is *not* consistent with change over time in *one and the same particular*. To see this, consider the fact that were Wiggins correct on this point, then it would be correct to identify a piece of coal with the living organism it once was.

Wiggins also makes a very useful distinction between what he calls "phase-sortals" and "substance-sortals," in maintaining a doctrine (with which I agree) called "essentialism." Essentialism is the view that there are no propertyless individuals (or, at the very least, that such individuals, such as Proteus, who could change into anything, are necessarily exceptional). What this means is that there must be a single concept under which a particular thing falls throughout its history, and the relevant concept must be something more detailed than, e.g., "material object" or "spatio-temporal continuant" (Aristotle's "prime matter"). Such concepts Wiggins calls substance-sortals. Examples would be "human being," "statue," "frog" and technical terms like "tachyon" or "Ecchinodermata" (a marine invertebrate). Phase-sortals, unlike substance-sortals describe only stages in the existence of a particular. Examples would be "infant," tadpole," "larva," etc. This distinction is also one we ordinarily make and must make for "practical purposes," but I think it is clear that it cannot be considered a "given" or "metaphysically ultimate." Another way of putting it would be to say that we have no way of knowing to what extent our division of reality into domains of particulars is dependent on our consciousness and pragmatic needs as opposed to existing independently of human beings. Everything develops out of something else; so that even *within* the conceptual scheme(s) which we presently employ it would be possible to deliberately invent a completely different set of substance-sortals which "redivide" the world in a new way. A more striking way of putting this would be to say that any substance-sortal we employ can ultimately, apart from certain pragmatic and scientific (or quasi-scientific) considerations, be treated as a phase-sortal in an all-inclusive substance. This is an (obscure) logical or conceptual reflection of the mystical assertion of the "unity of all things." The question naturally arises as to what this *one substance is*. That this question cannot be answered can be illustrated, I believe, by an ancient puzzle: take any two objects, A and B and "suppose" that all the properties of A (including spatio-temportal ones) become those of B and vice-versa. The oddity, of course, is that everything remains exactly the same: in one respect our "supposition" which appeared to have content, has none at all, for the "ultimate substance" which switches properties has, itself, no properties whatever. Thus the conclusion to which we are coherently led is itself almost incoherent; the one substance of which everything is a "phase" cannot apparently be described. Any allusion to it is "ineffable." I will now return to the question of the metaphysical relevance of the thesis that the identify relation is relative. In order to locate things in space it is necessary to specify a frame of reference. Where space is Euclidean and three-dimensional a frame of reference would consist abstractly of a point of origin and three axes at right angles to one another; to locate an object in space relative to this frame would then require three numbers, each representing a certain distance from the point of origin. A concrete example would be the following. Consider a large box, ten feet by ten feet and take a point in the centre of the box as the point of origin or our frame of reference. The vertical axis will be called y and the horizontal axes x and z; then, for example a point on the top surface of the box could be specified in this way: 5(x), 2(y) and 2(z). Now the crucial point for our purposes here is this. In order to locate real objects in actual space we must specify (tacitly or otherwise) a frame of reference, and in order to do this we must designate some point "in" or on the surface of a real object as the point of origin of the frame. This cannot be adequately done ostensively (i.e, by non-linguistic pointing) and given the theses above about the conceptual relativity of the cardinality of a domain and of identity, *the location of a point of origin for a frame of reference also becomes logically dependent on the concepts which we employ and how we employ them.* (e.g., to assert that the origin of the frame will be the centre of such and such an object obviously requires that we specify the relevant object and where the origin is located will depend on how we do this). Thus, precise spatial specifications and thus space itself, although not "unreal" in the sense that the concept of space is contradictory, is nonetheless "subjective" in this respect, that it is dependent on how we "arrange" the world by means of *our* concepts. In general the mechanism of this is obscure, but I hope this section has made one feature of it reasonably precise.

To summarize, what I hope to have established in this section is part of the logical or conceptual foundations of the "mystical" thesis that *reality* as we directly perceive and conceive it is not a "given." We can see logically that it is, to an important extent, *constructed by us,* but precisely to what extent and how we cannot see and hence we cannot "get at reality" by distinguishing (clearly) between the "given" and our own contribution to it. Objects and spatial relations are created by us, "from a single substance" that remains "ineffable."[13]

Notes to Chapter 6

1.   On this point see K. Popper's famous *The Logic of Scientific Discovery* (many editions).

2.   See the works of Wittgenstein previously cited and his *On Certainty* (Oxford: Blackwell's, 1969).

3.   There is a valuable and lengthy discussion of this point in S. Toulmin's *Wittgenstein's Vienna* (London: Weidenfeld and Nicolson 1973), which also includes further references.

4.   See Jones, ed., *The Private Language Argument*(London: MacMillan: 1971).

5.   See footnote 2 above.

6.   The failure to take this point seriously has, I believe, caused a lot of confusion, e.g., as when some philosophers ask whether the relationship between the criteria for the truth of a proposition and its truth is logical (i.e. *always* holds) or is contingent; it is logical but there are exceptions.

7.   See G. E. M. Anscombe, *Intention* (Oxford: Blackwell's 1972).

8.   P. T. Geach, *Mental Acts* (London: Routledge and Kegan Paul) (no date given).

9.   Another possibility, that platonism is true, will not be taken into account here since this would require another book in itself. (By "platonism" is meant the view that abstract concepts have an independent existence.)

10. P. T. Geach, "Identity," *Review of Metaphysics*, vol. XXI pp. 3-12.

11. Fritjof Capra, *The Tao of Physics* (Berkeley: Shambhala, 1975) p. 226.

12. For further references see my "Identity and Reference," *Mind*, Vol. LXXXII, N.S., No. 328 (October, 1973); pp. 542-556.

13. This is not to embrace "phenomenalism" (a view which I think can be adequately refuted by Wittgenstein's private language "argument"). On this see the excellent discussion in P. M. S. Hacker, *Insight and Illusion* (Oxford: Clarendon, Revised Edition, 1986) especially Chapter XI, Section 4.

CHAPTER SEVEN

The Unreality of Time

The purpose of this chapter is to explore certain problems about the idea of time which lead to the conclusion that the concept is really contradictory. If this is no, then the idealists were correct in making the paradoxical claim that time is unreal. Following McTaggart, the phrase "A-temporal determinations" will refer to the temporal "properties" of being past, present or future, and "B-determinations" to the temporal relations of being before, after or between. (I won't attempt to decide the question of what the relation between these two really is, but I will assume that, providing we have an absolutely reliable clock, we can dispense with the former. The point of this is to avoid the dispute about what real change really consists of, which seems to be irresolvable.)

I will first of all try to argue that it's impossible to construct a purely tenseness language which describes actual events. The purpose of this argument is twofold. Many philosophers, like Russell, Gruenbaum, Goedel and Smart who have been greatly influenced by the exact sciences have held some version of the thesis that B-time is real but that A-temporal properties are "subjective" or dependent on "consciousness of change" (the latter is Dummett's expression). Typically these philosophers have also held that it was possible to translate *every* meaningful tensed proposition into a tenseness one. The precise relation between these two doctrines is not altogether clear, but one possibility would be this. (A) *If* the idea that A-time is subjective is to have any real substance to it, it must be possible to construct a purely tenseless language. Whether this statement is true or false seems to depend on the sense of "subjective" involved. Among the many possible senses are these two, (1) illusory and (2) "real," but observer-dependent. The latter would include various metaphysical meanings but a very simple example will suffice for our immediate purposes here. If I say "You are over there" and "I'm here" then these statements can be objectively true, but they are obviously also observer-dependent. Now despite what some defenders of (A) above might say I don't think (A) is true where this latter sense of "subjective" is what is meant. I will give one reason for saying this here and another later. Let O-Space be the space described by words like "up," "here" and "there" and let (B) be the statement, "If O-Space is subjective it must be possible to construct a language which *locates* things in (real) Space without the use of O-spatial terms" (as opposed to just giving objects a spatial description). B is true but it's false that physical objects can be located in space without the use at some point of O-spatial terms. The reason for this is that, at some point, specifying a frame of reference (in a real world) will involve pointing, or the use of statements like "Let the center of the (i.e., *this*) earth be the point of origin." It follows, therefore, that (A) is true providing that "subjective" here means illusory in some respect. Hence if we can show that it's impossible to construct a tenseless language, then we will have shown that A-time is not some sort of universal illusion (unless time in general is). The second more important point of this argument opposing the view that we can construct a tenseless language then, is that it is impossible to specify temporal facts without the use of temporal indexical expressions. By an "indexical expression" will be meant a phrase whose essential occurrence in a sentence (essential in the sense that if the term were absent the meaning of the sentence would be different) makes that sentence capable of taking on different truth-values depending on the circumstances in which it is asserted, e.g., the time and place of its utterance, any pointing or other gestures with which it may be accomplished and so forth. The type of context governing the uses of these terms may be exceedingly complex as in the use of "he," "I," and "you." Other examples would be "here," "there" and "to the left of." Temporal examples are "now," "presently," "in the future" and the use of tenses (since, for instance, the truth-value of "It will rain in Toronto tomorrow" depends on when it is said). What I try to show first of all is that temporal indexical expressions or tenses cannot be logically disposed of, and that this shows that A-determinations are at least *as* fundamental as B-determinations.

This may hardly seem startling but I think in fact that the necessity for the use of temporal indexical expressions is quite mysterious. It is worth going into this here because it explains why the criticism of McTaggart's famous argument that time is unreal, that his argument simply muddles two ways of talking about time, tensed and untensed (or two types of change corresponding to these as Broad puts it), is insufficient. In general, the use of temporal indexical expressions is paradoxical in the following way. The consistency in the use of such terms depends on their obvious or covert reference to a relation between the user of the term and something else as in the case of 'here,' 'there,' 'I,' 'you,' and, exactly analogously, in the use of colour words. *Without* such an explanation the use of indexical terms would be contradictory (in a straightforward logical sense) for, e.g., one and the same person would be I (i.e., not you) and you (i.e., not I); the same side of an object could be left (i.e, not right) and right (i.e., not left). Of course this is not important in light of the facts, that we can in ordinary circumstances use these expressions without running into any logical difficulty, and we can very often give an explanation of this use to someone who finds it odd (e.g., to a child who cannot understand how both his head and that of a person on the other side of the world can be up). Even in cases such as that of the use of personal pronouns where it is quite difficult to give a philosophical account of what they refer to, there is no great difficulty in explaining how the same person can be both I and you, since on virtually any account more than one person exists and a person can refer to himself. What I will try to show is that in any language which can be used to talk about actual events there must be incorporated the distinction between past, present and future, and not just some means of indicating times that is logically independent of this distinction. This would require that such a language contain either indexical expressions *or* tenses or both. No *particular* statement in the language need contain either, but any statement about an event, state of affairs and so on in the language would depend for its intelligibility on the understanding of some statement containing indexical expressions or tenses. Such a language could be called "philosophically tensed."

The argument is simply this. In order to construct an (apparently) tenseless language one must specify a point of origin for the required time-scale and this can only be done by some such procedure as saying, "Let time O be now and set your watches accordingly" or "Let 1,988 years prior to now be time o, "etc. Having done this, and having a reliable clock, we can translate every proposition *but one* into a tenseless expression, but the former depend for their meaning on the latter; so that resulting language would not be "tenseless" in any philosophically interesting sense.

But a supporter of tenseless language might object that we can perfectly well imagine the user of this language employing only one calendar-watch that never went wrong. And to the question, "but what if it *did* go wrong?" replying that what the users of the tenseless language *mean* by "the correct date" is whatever date is indicated by this superchronometer. But suppose the clock stops. (It would be absurd to claim that this was a *logical* impossibility.) Are the users of the tenseless language then going to claim that all the events which occur until the clock starts up again are simultaneous? If they do, it hardly seems appropriate to call the statements in this language (as opposed to those in an ordinary tensed one) "observer-independent, scientific descriptions of reality."

It might also be objected that of course anyone would allow that in setting up the necessary calendar-clock, indexical expressions (or equivalent gestures, and so on) are required. The stopping of this chronometer simply means that this particular tenseless language-game has ceased to be operative and the conventions for starting it must be agreed on once again. Reading the correct time off calendar watches is a necessary part of the language; so of course some means of doing this must be available. But once these are provided, a language conforming to the standards of an "ideal scientific" one can function on its own. It is difficult to see offhand whether this gets us any further. It would mean, first of all, that the only mistake that *could* be made in the tenseless language with regard to dating an event would be a mistake in reading the time on a clock. But it would presumably be absurd to claim that a logically independent language whose special purpose was intended to be to reflect more clearly the "nature of reality," as opposed to our "subjective" view of it, *could not (logically) contain the statement that such and such a clock was not working properly, on the grounds that as soon as it was discovered that it was not, the language in question would cease to function.* We can put the point in this way: discovering that a watch wasn't working would amount to the introduction of the concept of the present "into the nlanguage" (though perhaps non-linguistically since what would be discovered would be that the time indicated on the watch wasn't now). Also, the fact that we *must* be able to talk of discovering that the clock does not work, and thus of having to *begin* the tenseless language-game again, indicates the "objective language" is not an independent one but *must* be a rather peculiar offshoot of a *tensed language.* There would have to be such a thing as a natural clock, not in the intelligible sense of some uniform repetition of events in nature to which numbers indicating times could be assigned, but an actual calendar-watch from which we could read off dates.

Intuitively there does seem to be an (obscure) respect in which events do "really" come before or after one another, but are not really past, present or future. We can now conclude, I think, that this intuition is mistaken. In this context no precise sense can be given to the "objective-subjective" distinction: saying that an event which does (or does not) fall under such and such a description, is past, present or future, is neither more nor less "objective" than saying that it is true or false that it *occurs.*

In the second part of this chapter I will take "subjective" to mean observer-dependent *and* relational. Given this interpretation I think it is false that the subjectivity of A-time entails that a tenseless language is impossible and, in fact, the former might even be used to explain the latter, perhaps by means of a very popular metaphysical picture which I will describe in a moment. The "subjectivity" in this sense of the "properties" of being here and, possibly, being to the left of, and so on, are very easily explained by showing how they are "produced" by *introducing an observer* into a spatial array of objects. Similarly, according to this metaphysical picture, "being now" and so on are "produced" by introducing an observer into a series of events. What is real is a four-dimensional space-time manifold the invariant intervals of which are spatio-temporal (not spatial or temporal) and causal: if E1 is a possible cause of E2 and E2 of E3 then we know that E2 is temporally between E1 and E3; *if* E2 is chosen as defining the "absolute now" of a particular frame of reference, then we know that E3 is absolutely future and E1 absolutely past *relative* to E2, but this has little, if anything, to do with the ordinary idea of the present, for these relations hold even if in *our* sense E is in the remote past or future. The manifold "as such" has no past or future. The latter is thought to be produced by consciousness in the following sense. (I will argue that this view is *not* correct.) Take the world line of any human being which exists, say, from time 0 to time 10. His consciousness comes into existence at time 0, "moves" (sic) up his world line to time 10 and then disappears. It is a peculiarity of human beings that they can only occupy a single temporal point at any given time and thus only "directly perceive" events (close by) at that time (or before that time for spatially remote events). Any two nows of beings who are spatially far apart may or may not be simultaneous relative to some third frame having a velocity relative to the first two. This, I think, is the basis of the idea that the Special Theory of Relativity supports the philosophical thesis that A-time is subjective. I will argue, however, that this idea is incorrect. What relativity establishes is not that such and such a time being *the present* depends on the existence of a conscious being, but only that if time 0 is the present here, then whether a certain time is also now to beings on a far distant planet does not admit of an absolute answer. It may seem too obvious to mention, but in a way it's important to remember, that it would be totally confusing to entertain the idea of two absolute nows *within a frame* being absolutely now *at the same time*, although that seems to be the only thing that corresponds exactly to the following: two spatially separate points can be both "here" (at a time) since *here* is "subjective." (Of course on *any* view two different times can be now *at a space*.) Thus the subjectivity of A-time does not, I believe, follow directly from relativity theory, but rather from a metaphysical picture which is based on it. I will now try to show why I think this picture is confused, i.e., why the use of "now" cannot be explained in the same way as the use of "here," or "to the left of." The first consideration is simply this. *One and the same object* can be on the left for you and not on the left for me although both of us are in the same frame of reference. But there is no possibility of the same time *within the same frame of reference* being now for you but past or future for me. One is inclined to say that, just as here is necessarily wherever I am, spatially, now is necessarily wherever I am temporally. But this is the wrong analogy: here is wherever I happen to be located, but (within a frame) we are *all necessarily* at the now temporally[1].

A second argument which is independent of considerations about relativity is this. It the idea that A-time is dependent on consciousness of change is really a conceptually possible thesis, then we ought to be able to explain how the introduction of an observer into a hypothetical time-series described, without the introduction of A-determinations, then enables us to divide that series into past, present and future. But consider a hypothetical series of events ...E1 to E5... which are temporally ordered but where none are specified as past, etc. It *looks as if* we can add A-time to this series by introducing an observer O who exists, say, from E2 to E4. But this, I think, is incorrect. All we can say is that E1 is "past," ie., *before* O's time and E5 is "future to O." But this "future to O" is really a B-determination, meaning, after the time of O's existence. *The crucial point is that we could say these sorts of things about ANY of the Es WITHOUT mentioning the observer.* Alternatively we might try saying, "Suppose that E2 is *now* present *to O.*" But *when* is it present? Either *now,* i.e., in *our* time, so that all we have done is relate the series to our time, or it is present *at* E2; but we can equally say that of any other of the observers' times by muttering the tautology "any time tn is always present at tn" and, again, simply of any of the times without the observer. Hence, all that is really being said is that events are present, when they are present but nothing about the supposed subjectivity of A-determinations has been shown. The correct "explanation," then, of why we can directly perceive only the present, appears to be that in some sense (which I cannot explain) only the present exists (if time exists at all).

In the first part of this chapter we found, or so I've claimed, that the description of temporal facts requires the use of (at least one) indexical expression and in the second part that the idea that A-time is observer-dependent (as opposed to being *just* relational) is incoherent. But this, I believe, is a paradox because the (usually simple) explanation of how an indexical expression (of the relevant sort) can be used without contradiction necessarily involves reference to a subject or observer. Thus the existence of time both does (part I) and does not (part II) require the existence of consciousness of change. The proper conclusion appears to be that the notion of time is contradictory and can no more be instantiated in reality than can the concept of the set of all sets which are not members of themselves.

There are at least the following objections to the idea that *any* argument could establish such a paradoxical conclusion. (1) To say that time is unreal is to say that there are no temporal facts. But a fact is what is stated by a true proposition; so if there are any true propositions involving "reference" to time, then time is real. Therefore, to say that time is unreal is to say concerning a very large class of propositions that, although the criteria for their truth is in each case satisfied, they are *really* false. But this is absurd. Therefore, the statement that time is unreal is nonsensical. A hint of Wittgenstein's sums up this sort of objection, I think. In *On Certainty* (section 114) he says, "If you are not certain of any fact, you cannot be certain of the meaning of your words either." (2) That time exists is so certain a fact that any "proof" of time's unreality must be less certain than the negation of the conclusion. A weird version of this might be that if the concept of time is contradictory so much the worse for logic; reality, must just *be* contradictory.
(3) The conclusion is self-refuting since the illusion of change is certainly real enough, but a *series* of illusions requires the existence of time, not an illusory time, but a real time.[2] This is *not* like the argument that an illusion of X is a real *illusion*, therefore it must have an object X in "some sense," but rather that an illusion of change is a *real change,* though not a change in a supposed object of observation, and therefore requires real time.

With respect to the first (perhaps Wittgensteinian) objection it is undoubtedly true that some philosophers have often been too eager to accepting the intelligibility of certain metaphysical statements, or in suggesting that we can genuinely understand a doubt raised about the criteria we actually employ, or in suggesting that we can genuinely understand alternative "conceptual schemes." Nonetheless, I think that arguments like this must be treated with great care or they *could* be used to prove, for instance, that Aristotelian matter and Absolute Time existed, since there used to be criteria for the "truth" of statements making reference to these things. (I do not mean to suggest that   Wittgenstein himself would argue in this way.) One must take a sort of intermediate position, I think, with respect to this sort of argument. The reply to the first and third objections would then be this. To claim that time is unreal is undoubtedly to reject a good deal of the conceptual scheme that we actually employ, but it does not involve the claim that we could *clearly* understand a conceptual scheme which described reality without the "erroneous" presupposition that time is real. We can perhaps understand the idea *that* time is unreal much as we could recognize *that* a system of gestures, sounds, written symbols, etc., was a system of communication (was "rational") while finding it impossible to either learn to use the system or to decipher the rules governing it[3] just as, to a slight extent, we can understand what it would be to perceive the world in a very different way from the way in which we do in fact perceive it, if, for example, we could see sound waves. To perceive reality atemporally would presumably be to "see" it as a static three-dimensional array. But how we could then experience our own emotional life is difficult if not impossible to explain, although perhaps Proust gives us a hint - any experience would now be "available" to direct experience. If time is unreal then a system of concepts which could be used correctly to describe reality would have to be consistent with Proust's suggestion. The second objection either begs the question or simply amounts to the psychological point that the conclusion that time is unreal is very hard to accept.

Appendix: Goedel's Argument

Kurt Goedel[4] has argued for the "subjectivity" of time in the following way. He points out that if the restricted theory of relativity is true, then it appears to be the case that time is relative but also objective, i.e., the temporal interval between two events occurring in frames of reference which have a velocity relative to one another is not an invariant quantity but depends on the frame of reference chosen, and is objective in that no reference to a conscious observer B is necessary. However, Goedel argues[5] that special relativity really entails that time is *subjective* for if we identify what exists with what *presently* exists, then (putting aside the question of "subjectivity" for the moment) the special theory of relativity would give us the result that *existence* is relative to a frame of reference which, according to Goedel, is obviously incoherent. He therefore concluded that the existence of time must be subjective, somehow ontologically dependent on an observer's consciousness of the series of events.

But surely Goedel's conclusion is at least as paradoxical as the idea that "existence is relative," especially in light of the fact that it is *impossible* according to the special theory to have the following situation: the temporal interval constituting the lifespan of a single object has a positive value relative to one frame and a zero value relative to another. In other words, according to the restricted theory, existence is an invariant although the temporal length of existence is not; and it seems that existence just can't be treated as only present existence within the theory, for surely *this* is relative on any account (of the special theory). It is possible, of course, for the temporal interval between two events to be positive relative to one frame and zero relative to another, but these events cannot occur to *one and the same individual*. In any case, the solution to Goedel's dilemma would seem to be to hold that B-time is real or "objective" (but relational); only A-time is subjective, and hence (as noted above), existence cannot be identified with present existence. Of course this may have been what Goedel meant (I would hesitate, to say the least, to either interpret or criticize his writings). I would then want to argue that the idea that B-time is real and A-time is "produced by our consciousness of change" is not really intelligible as I have tried to argue in the present chapter[6].

Notes to Chapter Seven

1.   This argument would have to be more complicated, if could be maintained at all, were time-travel physically possible in a way exactly analogous to ordinary travel in space.

2.   M. A. E. Dummett, "A Defense of McTaggart's Proof of the Unreality of Time," *Philosophical Review*, 69 (1960), p. 503.

3.   There is a valuable discussion of this idea in Barry Stroud's "Wittgenstein and Logical Necessity," *Philosophical Review*, 74 (1965), pp. 504-518.

4.   Kurt Goedel, "A Remark about the Relationship Between Relativity Theory and Idealistic Philosophy," in P. A. Schilpp, *Albert Einstein: Philosopher-Scientist* (Harper & Row, 1951), Vol. II, pp. 555-562.

5.   Ibid., p. 558, footnote 5.

6.   See also, T. Chapman, "Special Relativity and Idealism: A Remark on Goedel's Remark," *International Studies in Philosophy*, vol. XX, 1, 1988, pp.53 - 55

CHAPTER EIGHT

Wittgenstein's Epistemology and Omega-Inconsistency

The position that I try to argue for in this chapter is that it is possible to give an essentially very brief, and in some ways very simple, argument which suffices to refute any form of methodological or ontological skepticism or solipsism, but that one of our central ideas of knowledge is nonetheless paradoxical. In a way, phrases such as "skepticism" cover a wide range of philosophical positions, but they are all closely related in the following respect, that they are all animated by the genius of Descartes in that they take seriously the opening argument of his *Meditations*. As everyone knows, this argument claims to establish that it is possible to doubt the truth of any claim to knowledge whatever, except the truth of such propositions as "I think, therefore I am," and "I know with certainty that I think (something or other), correctly or incorrectly, and, therefore, I know with certainty that I exist." The argument for this conclusion, stated unadorned, is that no person can be absolutely certain that he is not now dreaming, in which case all of his beliefs are (probably) false except the belief that there exists a subject who is doing the dreaming. (A number of qualifications might have to be made, e.g., that it has only been established that there is dreaming going on, not that there is any subject who has the relevant thought. It has also been argued that the contradiction in "I do not exist" is performative, not logical, consisting in making the claim that one is having no thoughts. Fortunately, whether these refinements are necessary or not, does not effect our concerns here.)

The objection to this line of reasoning, based on some remarks of Wittgenstein in his book, *On Certainty*, is that if one can doubt anything then one can also incontestably doubt that one any longer understands the meanings of the words one is using.[1] But it immediately follows that one cannot claim to know indubitably at least one truth, e.g., "I exist," for in order to know that a statement is true one must, at the very least, understand its sense. As discussed in more detail below this consideration also throws some light on Wittgenstein's observation in the

Tractatus that what the solipsist intends is true, but it cannot be intelligibly stated. What is puzzling, however, is that it appears that the skeptic is obviously right in any particular case. What I mean is this: ordinarily we take all sorts of things for granted, as certainly true, and not just for practical purposes but for impractical ones as well.[2] Suppose, for example, (a) N says, "I told M about my trip this morning," and consider (b) "There are several books on my desk." In the first case we would be quite certain that what N says is true and ordinarily our only "evidence" for this would be that N says it, except in exceptional circumstances (N has a notoriously poor short-term memory, is quite mad, etc.). But suppose that we focus in, so to speak, on this particular statement and, especially, on what its truth implies. It implies, e.g., that N is not a very cleverly constructed robot, i.e., it entails all sorts of complex facts about human physiology, some of which are known and some not. Now it seems to be the case that if it is known that p implies q and it is unknown that q, then it is not known that p. Hence, it would seem to follow that without a very careful investigation which is never, in fact, carried out, we do not really know that statements like N's are true. One quickly loses patience with "philosophical" consideration of this kind: I'll come to the point shortly. In the case of (b), my books may have been replaced by those fake books which are really small safes by pranksters trying to show me that there's something in skepticism. Something very like this did happen to G. E. Moore when he was giving a lecture in defence of "common sense" at Harvard. He said that one of the things he knew with complete certainty was that there was sunlight coming through some overhead windows; in fact it was artificial light. The obvious retort here is that in the second case, easily, and in the first, with some difficulty, one can check as to whether or not one's doubts are justified, and, as Wittgenstein points out, these checks will come to an end. As Wittgenstein also argues, at some length and very convincingly in his *Philosophical Investigations*, where there is doubt there must at least be the possibility of knowledge. Hence, one cannot be properly said to know with absolute certainty that, e.g., one is or is not in pain since here, as in the case of may other inner psychic states, the concept of doubt has no intelligible application.[3] (On the other hand one can, for example, at least in exceptional cases, doubt that one really has such and such an intention since here self-deception is a real possibility.) I agree with Wittgenstein's arguments on this point but I intend to argue as well that the skeptic is nonetheless making an important and valid point which seems to reveal an important paradox in our concept of knowledge. What Wittgenstein's arguments establish, I believe, is that there are certain very general doubts which although they initially appear to make sense and even to have a methodological point, turn out (on the basis of a philosophical analysis) really not to make sense. It is important to note also that this can happen in several different ways. Consider the following: (i) I doubt that anyone is completely sane; (ii) I doubt that anyone (including myself) is awake; (iii) I suspect that all claims to knowledge are false; (iv) any claim to knowledge could be false. (v) I suspect that everyone (myself included) is totally mad. It's useful to compare (i) and (v); (i) might make some sort of sense providing one has at least a conceptual paradigm of what a perfectly sane person would be like. But (v) is clearly nonsensical: were it "true," then the person who uttered it would have to be mad himself and his statement selfrefuting. A similar point has often been made recently about claims like (ii) and (iii): in order to make statements about people being asleep one must understand the criteria for the truth of statements to the effect that someone is awake. If such criteria must sometimes be fulfilled (which seems the correct view but I won't try to establish that here), then (ii) is nonsensical. The same idea can be applied to the third example. What seems interesting to me, and makes clearer one of the points of skepticism, is that (iv) is true: we cannot as a matter of logic (in a broad sense of the term) doubt all claims to knowledge at once, but, as I tried to argue above, we can doubt any particular claim *in isolation.* In a way this makes Descartes' example especially interesting. He may be right that each of us, at least on any occasion we are alone, can doubt his or her own sanity and, therefore whether or not he or she knows anything at all- or, rather, which of the things that he thinks he knows he really does know. However, we could still have the situation that such a person could not articulate his doubts or certainties (e.g., of his own existence) with any confidence. It is only the fact that we are social beings and that language is necessarily public which undermines one version of skepticism.

I will try to illustrate this idea further by a discussion of some of the views of a distinguished contemporary philosopher who at one time denied it. Norman Malcolm[4] takes the view (like Moore) that there are all sorts of propositions, the truth of which cannot be coherently doubted. His argument for this (or rather my attempted reconstruction of it) is that to understand a fragment of a language is, in part, to understand the criteria for the truth of certain propositions. Often we know that these criteria are fulfilled. But in such cases, to doubt the truth of the corresponding proposition is simply logically incoherent. Hence, there are all sorts of things of which we are absolutely certain. Recalling the example mentioned above of the books (or false books) on my desk, we can easily satisfy ourselves eventually that they are or they are not fake. The case of reports of a person's inner mental life are more difficult, but the same observation seems, at least, to apply.

There appear to be two quite different types of reply that the skeptic can make to Malcolm's type of argument. (1) The criteria for the truth of many beliefs commonly thought to be known are extremely complicated, obscure and open-ended. This is true to such a degree that I doubt in many cases that we can say whether we know these criteria are, in fact, fulfilled or not. (2) In any particular case the skeptic can legitimately raise a philosophical or "contextual" objection to any claim to (certain) knowledge. (This is explained below.) With regard to (1) the example given after (a) on the second page of this chapter will serve. Such a statement presupposes, amongst other things, the existence of persons, and I think everyone would agree that its impossible to give a complete and precise list of the exact criteria for the truth of any proposition about persons. It might be objected right off, somewhat dogmatically and even paradoxically, that something has obviously gone wrong, since it simply is the case that we all know many propositions about persons to be true. Certainly Moore would say this. But what this objection amounts to is that there is a kind of knowledge for which "Knp -> Kn(Knp)" (if p is known then it is known that p is known) is false. What I mean is this: ordinarily (or in an ordinary "sense" of "knowledge") there are all sorts of things such that we know them, but do no know *that* we know them or precisely why we know them. This is one way of interpreting "Knp -> Kn(Knp)" as sometimes false. As already mentioned this would be true of any proposition involving reference to persons.   Another example would be that of a schoolboy who understands the Pythagorean Theorem and knows that it's true but has forgotten any proof of it. Now the skeptic can rightly claim that there is a kind of knowledge, "philosophical" if you wish, in which "Knp -> Kn(Knp)" is true, a kind of *real* knowledge where one also knows what the basis of the knowledge is, where its grounds are conscious and explicit.[5]   Relative to this sort of knowledge one only knows that statements about persons are true if one can spell out the criteria of personal identity over time, and the schoolboy knows Pythagoras' Theorem only if he can construct a proof of it.   Example (b) on the second page is of a different sort, since clearly here one can easily satisfy oneself that the criteria of truth are satisfied. But here too the skeptic can raise doubts of a more general but not completely general kind. These can be of various sorts. (a) I might doubt my own sanity while viewing the books. This, of course is not the same as doubting the sanity of everyone all the time. And I could give reasons for this doubt (even if only of an abstract kind, e.g., that people really have been deluded in such circumstances) and these doubts might turn out to be justified, e.g., if I were to wake up later in a mental hospital, etc. (b) Such general doubts might be of a more philosophical kind. What I have in mind here is based on a remark of Wittgenstein's that our ordinary beliefs rest on or imply very general and abstract beliefs, which might be called "metaphysical," that are very rarely explicitly spelled out except by philosophers such as Kant. An example of such a belief in the book-example would be this. (c) "The spatial separation (individuation) and spatial characteristics of (macroscopic) physical objects persist long enough temporally for us to distinguish and count the objects in question." *Providing certain other things remain true, so that we can understand how to speak or think at all,* the skeptic appears to be right that we could doubt that this particular metaphysical belief will hold long enough for us to know that the statement about books which implies it, is true. A. J. Ayer makes what I take to be a similar point in an interesting way when he says, "so long...as we are operating within [a] theory [I would prefer something like "world-view"] the margin which is allowed for error, though always present, is vanishingly small."[6] The skeptic's point is that it is *always present* and so, in one respect, Moore and Malcolm are wrong. (I do not mean that their positions are identical.) The respect in which they are right is that there are sets and probably subsets of propositions such that we cannot doubt all of them at once without lapsing into speechlessness.

As an aid to seeing the apparent upshot of all this let us consider first of all the following simple example. We have ten cards labelled 1 to 10, one of which is to be drawn out of a hat to determine a prize. Let $p1$ be the statement "1 is the winning number," $p2$ be the statement "2 is the winning number," and so on. $Db(p1)$ will mean, it is reasonable to doubt the truth of $p1$ which (for our purposes here) means the same as, it's not provable (knowable) that $p1$, expressed as $\sim Prov(p1)$ and $\sim Kn(p1)$. (The notion of provability here is not, of course, necessarily formal, though it could be in some cases.) Now there is a perfectly good sense in which, even prior to the draw, it is true that each of the p's is doubtful and yet is wrong to formalize this as $(Ap)\sim(Provp)$, ie., $\sim(Ep)(Provp)$, using A for the universal quantifier and E for the existential where p ranges over the propositions in question, since certainly one of these propositions is provable (after the draw). But clearly in this case an alleged "paradox" in the fact that each of the p's is doubtful and yet (Ap) $(\sim Provp)$ *is false* has no significance. Hence, it might be claimed that, exactly analogously, no significance attaches to what I have alleged to be true about skepticism, that each of a set of propositions may be doubted but not the whole set. However, I mention this example to illustrate that the comparison is not legitimate. For part of the point, in the purely epistemological cases, is that (in a certain respect) it must be possible for all the propositions under consideration to be true at once. Hence, it is not like the above simple probabilistic case but more like this one. Let $p1$ be: "It's doubtful that he knows Gaelic" and the p's amount to "It's doubtful that he knows any Slavic language." From this it obviously does follow that Db (he knows Gaelic) *and* Db (he knows Polish) and etc., i.e., (Ap)Db(p). To say the latter is false would yield a paradox. But what sort of paradox is not yet clear; so we need a better analogy.

I think a better analogy is provided in the formal logician's concept of omega-consistency. It is sometimes possible to uniquely specify any formula of a formal system by means of its Goedel number and thus, to prove certain things through substitution and manipulation of the numbers of the formulas rather than the formulas themselves. In the general case of interest here let $N(k)$ be the numeral representing k in a formal system A, and let h be the number of a formula H(n), then the assertion that all the formulae H(1), H(2),....H(n)...are provable is expressed by $(Ak)(Em)Prov\ St_h(v/\ N(k))$. This means: for all k, there exists an m, such that the formula numbered m constitutes a proof of the formula obtained by substituting the numeral $N(k)$ for the variable numbered v in the formula numbered h. As Goodstein points out, this may be provable though H(n) is not and amounts to "a formalization of the notion of an arbitrarily assigned integer."[7] The example can be explained informally in the following way. It may be possible in a formal system FS to prove that each of F(0), F(1)...is provable without being able to prove (Am) F(m) where m ranges over the positive integers; the Goedel number of the latter will be different from that of the former, so in that (formal) sense they are not " of any of F(1), F(2), etc., is not that of (Em) Fm. Hence, it is even possible to have a formal system where we have a formula (viz, the one mentioned above) which expresses the fact that each of F(0), F(1)... is provable, but where (Em) ~Prov F(m) is also provable. Such a system is said for propositions, we have both that each of F(0), F(1), etc. is true (by the argument in defence of skepticism) and that (Em)~Fm is also true (by the epistemological argument based on Wittgenstein's writings).

One conclusion that can be drawn from this is that, despite appearances, we do not have a coherent idea of "respectable" scientific or protoscientific empirical knowledge with which dubious "mystical" knowledge is to be contrasted.

A last question which arises is this: should we say that those ordinary propositions which can be doubted are *necessarily exceptional*? If the answer to this question is "yes" our whole position seems to be undermined since skepticism is applicable only in odd cases and this is something that everyone would grant in any case. But "yes" is the wrong answer to the question for the following reason. Any empirical proposition is open to some sort of possible doubt: it is an "exceptional case" (when doubting occurs) only in the sense that if p is the claim being doubted, then, on that occasion, there must, as a matter of logic, be a large class of propositions, general and particular, which are not being doubted. Therefore, all that follows is that skepticism is necessarily a rare state of mind (from a rational, not psychological, point of view), not that any particular proposition is immune from doubt.

Notes to Chapter Eight

1.	Wittgenstein, *On Certainty*, eds., G. E. M. Anscombe and G. H. von Wright (Oxford: Basil Blackwell, 1969). Sections 114, 369, 456-507. In 383 he says: "The argument 'I may be dreaming' is senseless for this reason: if I am dreaming, this remark is being dreamed as well - and indeed it is also being dreamed that these words have any meaning." (p. 49e.)

2.	Cf. Wittgenstein, Section 519: "But since a language game is something that consists in the recurrent procedures of the game in time, it seems impossible to say in any individual case that such-and-such must be beyond doubt if there is to be a language game - though it is right enough to say that as a rule some empirical judgment or other must be beyond doubt." (p. 68e.) Cf. D. Odegard, *Knowledge and Skepticism*, (Totowa, New Jersey: Rowman and Littlefield, 1982), Chapter VII. Professor Odegard disagrees with Wittgenstein on some other points however.

3.	On the incoherence of the idea of a private language see L. Wittgenstein's *Philosophical Investigations*, especially Part 1, pp. 243-315 and 348-412. For discussions of these texts see e.g., George Pitcher, ed., *Wittgenstein: The Philosophical Investigations* (London: Macmillan, 1968) and P. M. S. Hacker, *Insight and Illusion* (Oxford: Clarendon, Revised Edition, 1986).

4.	See, e.g., his paper, "Moore and Wittgenstein on the sense of 'I know,'" in his book *Thought and Knowledge* (Ithaca and London: Cornell University Press, 1977).

5.	Cf. Odegard, Chapter VIII.

6.	A.J. Ayer, "Wittgenstein on Certainty," in *Understanding Wittgenstein* (Macmillan, 1974).

7.	R. L. Goodstein, "The Significance of Incompleteness Theorems," in his book *Essays in the Philosophy of Mathematics* (Leicester University Press, 1965), p. 159.

CHAPTER NINE

Persons

If twentieth-century analytical philosophy has established anything, it is that many philosophical problems arise out of various types of
linguistic confusion and can be resolved by what on the surface at least
appear to be grammatical investigations. A closely-related point is that
many philosophical problems *and* their solutions lie in the narrow range
of intellectual enquiry separating, in a fragile manner, the ludicrous from
the profound. As Wittgenstein remarked, a good philosophy text could
be written which consisted entirely of jokes. Such considerations apply
particularly to the issues to be considered in the present chapter. The
question I propose to tackle is, "What are persons?" and the method of
enquiry will be to try to answer the seemingly grammatical question,
"What is the reference or denotation of the pronoun 'I'?" Unfortunately,
this will require constant reference to myself! I hope the reader will
forgive the apparent egoism: it can be avoided if the reader will simply
understand the reference to be to herself or himself. The use of 'I,' it will
emerge, as opposed to some other pronoun, is inessential to the
argument.

The above question is only *seemingly* grammatical in the following
respect. The answer that we finally arrive at can hardly be said to be an
answer to the question: What ultimately, must persons be, whether we
consciously realize that we are referring to such subjects or not?

In a deep and fascinating paper, Professor G. E. M. Anscombe[1] has
argued that the first person pronoun is not a referring expression at all
and in this she has been supported in an analysis of her paper by
Professor Norman Malcolm.[2] Similar arguments can be found in
Professor Sprague's book on metaphysics.[3] It is rather difficult to give a
useful, explicit definition of the phrase "referring expression" but the
central idea can be conveyed by means of examples. A referring
expression is any term which either has as its meaning the object to
which it refers, or, more plausibly, gets its meaning *in virtue of* referring
to some definite object or subject, e.g., the proper names of human

beings like "Norman Malcolm," numerals like "two," and definite descriptions such as "the one and only positive square root of the integer twenty-five" and "the one and only President of the United States in 1988." (This use of "referring expression" creates a problem, or apparent problem, which, fortunately, we need not resolve for purposes of the present chapter, viz., that there are referring expressions which have meaning but no reference, e.g., "the present king of Italy"). Although I agree with the substance of Miss Anscombe's arguments, at least to the extent to which I understand them, it does not seem to me that they necessarily lead to the conclusion that 'I' has no reference. Rather they seem to establish that the first person pronoun does not refer to what we might think that it does on the basis of fairly common-sensical considerations. However, having acknowledged my indebtedness to the work of Anscombe, Malcolm and Sprague I will not pretend to be interpreting their arguments but will simply present arguments which seem to me to be right.

In one way the question, "What does 'I' refer to?" is extremely easy to answer: it refers to that very person who is using the word 'I' in such sentences (true or false) as "I have six children" or "I am not at present riding a bicycle." The question then, of course, is precisely what we mean by "human person" and generally speaking this question too does not lead to insurmountable problems for ordinary, legal and moral purposes. Nonetheless, the criteria of personhood we actually employ are complex, sometimes rather vague and certainly do not provide exact answers in all, especially borderline, cases. For this reason, the search for the *the* criterion of personhood presupposed by "ordinary language" or "the reasonable man" appears to be futile. Sometimes for example, memory provides the criterion, sometimes the spatio-temporal continuity of a particular body. And it's fairly easy to imagine cases where we would not know *what* to say, e.g., were "a" person to pop in and out of existence but claim to be that very person who had existed at previous times, had accurate memories of his previous experiences, and so on. Or again, and more in accord with common experience, we may be hard pressed in the case of Siamese twins to say whether we have two persons who share bodily parts or one person with an extended body; or in the case of a human being who has changed very radically both physically and with respect to his personality through, say, religious conversion, whether or not "he" has become a completely different person.

From one point of view human beings are a species of animal possibly different from other species in two main respects, in our ability to use languages for communication with each other which are more complex than the languages of other animals and in our being conscious of ourselves, able to use reflexive pronouns and able to construct languages containing self-referential expressions. But there are, of course, many other biological facts of some significance and also certain grammatical and metaphysical ones. We refer to each other using a great many different types of expression including proper names which I will simply express by the abbreviations "N," "EA," "TC," "NM," etc. If you are N then the proposition "I am N" is true for you (and for me!) if the proposition is uttered by you, i.e., if the performance of uttering the proposition is made by the right person. However, as Miss Anscombe very strikingly argues, the expression 'I' and 'N' even for one and the same person function in very different ways. Suppose you say, "I am Nellie McNellman (=N)." The reference of "I" in such a statement is *guaranteed.* In a way it is a very odd fact that *necessarily* you succeed in referring to the right person. You may not, of course, actually *be* Nellie McNellman but under the illusion that you are, in which case the above statement is false but *not* because you have failed to correctly refer to the right person by "I"; but precisely because you have *succeeded* and are not Nellie McNellman. This suggests the first significant fact about persons: *if* "I" is a referring expression then there is at least one person that a person cannot fail to correctly pick out, denote, or refer to, viz., himself or herself, even where that person's conception of herself or himself is grossly delusive. Because of the latter, this metaphysical truth is *not* based on the fact that we have any special (e.g., introspective) *knowledge* of ourselves although we can certainly be conscious or not conscious of ourselves.[4] And in fact our knowledge of ourselves (both individually and as a species) is rather jejune; often a person knows less about himself than (say) his spouse. Yet each person apprehends himself in a unique way: he does not know himself nor *what* he is any more than he has a special sort of knowledge of his own private experience.[5] *Each metaphysical subject just is the subject of his own experience.* And the only way of being certain that one is referring to this subject is by means of the expression "I" or something equivalent. If the word "I" does *not* refer, then what I have just said could be construed as arising out of a kind of illusion created by the forms of our language. This seems to be what Miss Anscombe has in mind by her intriguing remark, "In the thought 'The *I* was subject not object, and hence invisible,' we have an example of language itself being as it were possessed of an imagination, forcing its image upon us."[6] This image does not seem to be entirely misleading. I do not mean by this that I pretend that I can show that Miss Anscombe is wrong in arguing that the word "I" has no reference at all, but only that it is possible to use a certain interpretation of her arguments to suggest that *either* "I" has no reference, or that it has a reference very remote from that which commonsense would ascribe to it.

Following Miss Anscombe it is fairly easy to see that the usual answers that philosophers have attempted to give to the problem of the denotation of "I" are not adequate. Two or three examples will suffice to show this. A person's causal connections to a particular body are peculiarly intimate (and various): one can only *directly* move the limbs, change the position, etc., of one's own body. However, the word "directly" here does not *explain* anything, but involves a tautology; relatively slight changes in one's neurophysiological balance can result in psychosis, etc. However, it appears almost obvious that the reference of "I" is not *identical with* the body: a person can be anesthetized in such a way as to be conscious (of the "external world") and self-conscious but have no awareness of his body. It is perfectly meaningful for a person in such a state to say, "I wonder if I still have a body" which can hardly mean, "I wonder if my body still has a body." In general, any person can fairly easily imagine being causally disconnected from the physical world altogether and to be simply observing it through a metaphysical glass with no body at all. I mean we can imagine this being so as a *necessarily exceptional* case, given Wittgenstein's and others' powerful arguments that our ways of using concepts to do with human persons is inextricably involved with descriptions of physical behavior. Similarly, the *identification* of oneself with the mind, soul (in one sense), or, the substance of introspective experience, is also easily seen to be wrong by simply observing the possible truth of such statements as "Yesterday I stubbed my toe" which can hardly be translated into, "Yesterday my soul stubbed its toe". If "I" is a referring expression, an answer somewhat like Descartes' might be correct, but, as many philosophers have pointed out, it is open to the following insuperable objection, that if the self is to be identified with the subject of introspective experience, infallibly denoted as one utters the incantation "cogito ergo sum," then there is no reason to reject the idea that there may be as many selves inhabiting a body as there are introspective acts confirming its (or their) existence. As Hume and Kant[7] pointed out, there does not seem to be any grounds for the claim that one *knows* one's introspective self as a continuous existent through time. I am inclined to say, although I cannot substantiate this, that everyone *does* know this to be the case even when she or he is in doubt as to whether an alleged memory is really a memory of her/his experience; but surely, even if we know this, we do not know *how* we know it and its connections with *direct* experience and the experience of time, if there is such a thing, or at least change, is very obscure. It is, of course, possible to "relive" one's own past and occasionally future experience in a very vivid way and to wonder whether or not it really was the same person who had this experience and to wonder at the fact that one can "have" such wonders and such doubts. It is certainly right to say that our idea of *experience* is an idea of something inherently temporal and that in the case of *some* experiences, at least, they are not *themselves* continuous, but strung together in discrete units. This is not in itself paradoxical although its connection with the mathematical time of physical theory is not altogether clear. What *is* deeply mysterious is the connection of human experience to the obscure, but undeniable, fact,, that *the present seems* (at least) to have a special ontological status.[8] This appears to entail an absurdity of the kind that St. Augustine discusses, viz., that the only events that we can "directly perceive" are those which "occupy" *the now* (or, given the finite velocity of light, perhaps we should say, that occupy an instant just prior to *the now*). But, of course, this sort of event is just precisely what we cannot perceive directly or otherwise since such an event is of infinitesimal length. This might tempt us to try to introduce a phenomenal or mental time different from that of the time employed in physical models, but I shall not pursue this idea here as I have tried to demonstrate elsewhere, that this idea is not a fruitful one but simply creates more problems about the relations of time and perception.[9] Further difficulties arise if we attempt to *count* selves at a time. For practical and other purposes we usually do this through counting bodies, but if we were to employ a more Cartesian method we might conclude that there are many selves "inside" a single body, e.g., an agent-self,[10] a self which is aware of the former, another self which is aware of the (first) thinking self, and so on. Or we might conclude, or at least conjecture, the opposite, viz., that there are not really several selves, even dispersed amongst several bodies, but just *one* which we mistakenly perceive as our own. (There are psychiatric and anthropological analogues of both these situations: multiple personalities and, apparently, examples of "primitive" people who do not clearly differentiate themselves from the clan to which they belong.) The conclusion that is realistically forced upon us is not *in itself* "realistic" or even plausible, but, is, given the evidence, *true*. It is that the self in the sense of the metaphysical subject of experience, does not endure through space and time closely casually linked to a particular organism (or identical with it) but that it is "connected" to such an organism and to spacetime in an *inexplicable* way. (This idea, like certain mathematical theorems, is forced upon us by an inexorable logic without the theorem itself even having any clear meaning.) The self cannot be *in time* in this respect, of being *at* the present for the reasons given above concerning infinitesimal chronons, nor can it be *in time* in the sense of spread out in (space-) time for this would make our past and future experience, or part of it, as immediate to us as our present experience. Nor is it at all clear what the properties of the self *are*, other than being the subject of experience. It is very easy to ridicule such a conclusion; it is much harder to explain why it does not follow. It appears much more "realistic" and even "logical" to conclude that there is no such thing as the metaphysical subject of experience (to give up the idea of the "transcendental ego" as some phenomenologists did). Hume claimed, quite rightly, that he failed to come across the subject of experience, metaphysical or otherwise, through introspection. All he could discover was the experience itself. But to conclude from this, which procedure is almost universal amongst analytical philosophers, that the self as subject of experience does not exist because its properties are not obviously present to our awareness, seems in itself slightly comical. Even an extreme materialist who claimed that he "just" was his body would nonetheless admit that his knowledge of it was very inadequate. To try to "analyze" the notion of a person through an analysis of "ordinary language" is useful as a first step but as an attempt to grasp the nature of the actual "thing" in question it is as ludicrous as the attempt to understand matter through an analysis of the word in ordinary speech. In the *Tractatus* Wittgenstein says "that in an important sense there is no subject . ...(5.631) The subject does not belong to the world: rather, it is a limit of the world (5.632)," just as the eye is not part of the visual field. If Wittgenstein did think that the subject did exist in (another) sense, he apparently did not think that it was something that could be significantly talked about: its existence and nature can only be shown. This is very close to the conclusion of this chapter though, I doubt that Wittgenstein would approve of this attempt to talk about it.

We have seen that the self is, in a way, timeless. It also, in a way, has no location but is, to use Wittgenstein's analogy like a limit, or the point from which the metaphysical field is experienced, just as the eye is the point from which the visual field is seen. We have found no reason to suppose that the metaphysical subject is a countably distinct entity which is different for each human being. Nor is it normally an object of experience, introspective or otherwise, direct or indirect. But there are people who occasionally have enjoyed mystical experiences which could be interpreted as direct experiences of the metaphysical subject. Thus Proust says: "The being that had been reborn in me when, with so great a quiver of happiness, I heard a noise that was common both to a spoon touching a plate and to a hammer striking against a wheel, to the unevenness, perceptible to the feet, both of the Guermantes quadrangle and the baptistery of St. Mark's, - that being feeds on nothing but the essence of things, in them alone it finds its subsistence and its delight. ... It suffices that a sound once heard before, or a scent once breathed in, should be heard and breathed again, simultaneously in the present and the past, real without being actual, ideal without being abstract: then, immediately, the permanent essence of things which is usually hidden, is set free, and our real self, which often had seemed dead for a long time yet was not dead altogether, awakes and comes to life as it receives the heavenly food now proffered to it. One minute delivered from the order of time creates in us, that we may enjoy it, the man delivered from the order of time. How easy to understand that this man should be confident in his joy, even if the mere taste of a bun may not seem, logically, to contain within itself the reasons for that joy. It is understandable that the word "death" can have no meaning for him: situated, as he is outside time, what could he fear from the future? Instead of taking a more flattering view of my ego, I had, on the contrary, almost doubted the actual reality of the ego."[11]

There is, of course, an empirical self which is or has a personality and can be an object of observation, ordinary, introspective and even scientific. This self as part of the world can be itself "perceived", known about, by the real self, which is very rarely itself directly perceived, but exists, not as one amongst several entities but outside space and time.

We (each of us) might conclude by observing that we know from the outside, so to speak, that we are a certain species of animal, each with a distinctive character and personality, very imperfectly understood both from a psychological and physiological point of view. And any person can make herself/himself an object of study from these various points of view. But all such information is *contingent*: it is as if we are *necessarily* something, especially when our object of study is our own selves, but we cannot say precisely what this is, nor individuate it. If we exchange metaphysical selves, everything, in a way, remains the same. So it would be natural to reject the whole idea on positivist grounds, as many philosophers have, were it not for certain occasional and joyful experiences (which could also be explained in other ways). But there is the fact of *self*-consciousness, of reason closely correlated with it and the following, very ordinary sort of experience: a number of people are contemplating the summer sky over a lake just before sunset; for a captured moment we all have the same experience, just as people a hundred years ago did and a hundred years hence will, it is hoped, perhaps in the same place, but this too seems irrelevant. It is a difficult point to argue but it seems highly artificial here to insist that we can in this situation count various selves, time and places.[12] But we can here *allude* to something, as I have tried to argue in this chapter, which is not clearly expressible, but is of the utmost importance.

Notes to Chapter Nine

1. G. E. M. Anscombe, "The First Person," in S. Guttenplan, ed., *Mind and Language* (Oxford University Press, 1975), pp. 45-66.

2. N. Malcolm, in *Essays for G. E. M. Anscombe*, ed. Cora Diamond, (Cornell University Press, 1980).

3. E. Sprague, *Metaphysical Thinking* (Oxford University Press, 1978), Section 2.

4. Anscombe, pp. 64, 65.

5. L. Wittgenstein, *Philosophical Investigations*, Sections 220-250 and *passim*.

6. Anscombe, p. 59.

7. Cf. also I. Kant's *Critique of Pure Reason*, transl. Norman Kemp Smith (London: MacMillan, 1958 (Riga, 1787)), pp. 245-252 and 368-381.

8. C. F. K. Goedel, "A Remark about the Relationship between Relativity Theory and Idealistic Philosophy," *Albert Einstein: Philosopher-Scientist*, ed. P. A. Schilpp (New York: Harper and Row, 1951), vol. II, pp. 555-562.

9. T. Chapman, *Time: A Philosophical Analysis* (Dordrecht Reidel, 1982), pp. 80-82.

10. Anscombe, p. 52.

11. Proust, pp. 872-873. Zaehner's translation.

12. Cf. E. Schroedinger in Section 10 of K. Wilber, ed., *Quantum Questions* (Boulder & London: Shambhala, New Science Library, 1984) pp. 95-97.

BIBLIOGRAPHY

Anscombe, G. E. M. *Intention*, (Oxford: Basil Blackwell 1963, Second Edition).

Ayer, A. J. "Wittgenstein on Certainty," in *Understanding Wittgenstein*, (London: MacMillan, 1974).

Bochenski I. M. "On Analogy," in A. Meen, ed., *Logico-Philosophical Studies*, (Dordrecht, Holland: Reidal, 1962,) pp. 97 - 117.

Capra, F. *The Tao of Physics*, Berkeley: Shambhala, 1975)

Chapman, T. "Identity and Reference," *Mind*, LXXXII, (N. S. Oct. 1973,) pp. 542-556

Chapman T. "Special Reletivity and Idealism: A Remark on Goedel's Remark," *International Studies in Philosophy*, Vol XX, I, 1988, pp. 53 - 55.

Chapman, T. *Time, A Philosophical Analysis*, (Dordrecht, Holland: Reidel, 1982).

Diamond, C. *Essays For G. E. M. Anscombe*, (Ithica N.Y.: Cornell University Press, 1978).

Dummett, "A Defense of McTaggart's Proof of the Unreality of Time," *Philosophical Review*, 69, 1960. pp. 502 - 511

Frege, G. *Logical Investigations*, ed., P. T. Geach, (Oxford: Blackwell's 1977).

Geach, P. T. "Identity," *Review of Metaphysics*, XXI September, 1967) pp. 3 - 12.
Geach, P. T. *Mental Acts*, (London: Routledge & Keagan, no date given)

Goedel, K. "A Remark About the Relationship Between Reletivity Theory, and Idealistic Philosophy", in P. A. Schilpp, *Albert Einstein: Philosopher Scientist* (New York: Harper & Row, 1951) pp.555 - 562.

Goodstein, R. L. " The Significance of Incompleteness Theorems," in his *Essays in the Philosophy of Mathematics,* (Leicester University Press, 1965).

Guttenplan, S. ed., *Mind and Language,* (Oxford University Press, 1975).

Hacker, P. M. S. *Insight and Illusion,* (Oxford: Clarendon Press, 1986).

Happold, F. C. *Mysticism,* (Harmondsworth, Middlesex: Penguin, 1970).

Hartshorne, C., "The Logic of Ontological Argument" in W. Rowe & W. Wainwright, eds. *Philosophy of Religion,* (New York: Harcourt, Brace, Jovanovich, 1973).

Kant I., *Critique of Pure Reason,* trans. Norman Kemp Smith, (London: MacMillan, 1958).

Katz, S. T. ed., *Mysticism and Philosophical Analysis,* (London: Sheldon Press, 1978).

Kenny, A., ed., *Aquinas: A Collection of Critical Essays,* (London: MacMillan, 1969).

Malcolm, N., "Anselm's Ontological Arguments" in his *Knowledge and Certainty,* (Ithaca, New York: Cornell University Press, 1963).

Murdoch, I., *The Sovereignty of Good,* (London: Routledge & Kegan, 1970).

Odegard, D., *Knowledge and Skepticism* (New Jersey: Rowan and Littenfield, 1982).

Phillips, D. Z., "Religious Beliefs and Language Games" *Ratio*, 12 (1970) pp. 26 - 46.

Plantinga, A., ed., *The Ontological Argument*, (Garden City, New York: Doubleday, 1965).

Reichenbach, H., *The Direction of Time*, (University of California Press, 1970).

Scharfstein, B., *Mystical Experiences*, (Harmondsworth, Middlesex: Penguin, 1974).

Stroud, B., "Wittgenstein and Logical Necessity," *Philosophical Review*, 74, 1965, pp. 504 - 518.

Thomas, J. E., "On the Meaning of Analogy is Analogous" *Theologique et Philosophique* (Laval), XXII, 1, 1966, pp. 73 - 79.

Toulmin, S., *Wittgenstein's Vienna*, (London: Weidenfeld and Nicolson, 1973).

Wilber, K., ed, *Quantum Questions*, (London: Shambala, New Science Library, 1984).

Wittgenstein, L., *On Certainty* (Oxford: Blackwell's 1969).

Wittgenstein, L., *Philosophical Investigations*, (Oxford: Blackwell's, 1967, Second Edition).

Wittgenstein, L., *Tractus Logico-Philosophicus*, (London: Routledge and Kegan)

Zaehner, R. C., *Mysticism Sacred and Profane* (Oxford University Press, 1969).

Index

PROBLEMS IN CONTEMPORARY PHILOSOPHY